The Illustrated Encyclopedia of
AVIATION

Volume
2

Reference edition published 1979

Reference edition © 1979 Marshall Cavendish Limited
© Orbis Publishing Limited 1977

Printed in Great Britain

Bound in the United States

Library of Congress Cataloging in Publication Data
Main entry under title:

The Illustrated encyclopedia of aviation.

First published in 1977 under title: Wings.
Includes index.
1. Aeronautics—History. I. Robinson, Anthony,
1947—
TL515.144 1979   629.13'009   78—12408
ISBN 0—85685—318—6 (set)
ISBN 0—85685—575—8 (vol 2)

Picture Acknowledgements

Cover: James Gilbert—121: Hawker Siddeley—122:
Popperfoto; Imperial War Museum—123: W/C K.H.
Wallis—124-25: W.B. Klepacki; J. Jahr—126: W.B.
Klepacki—127: Imperial War Museum—128: E.G. Gee
—128-29: E.G. Gee; H.J. Nowarra—129: E.G. Gee—130-
31: Imperial War Museum—131: Imperial War Museum
—132: Shuttleworth Collection; Chaz Bowyer—133: D.J.
Kingston; Flight International—134: Flight International
—134-35: Chaz Bowyer—135: Hawker Siddeley—136: Crown
Copyright; Bruce Robertson—136-37: Fox—138-39: J.W.
Wood—139: Bruce Robertson—140: Ministry of Defence;
Bruce Robertson—141: Fox—142: Fox— 142-43: IWM;
Fox—143: IWM—144: Philip Moyes—144 -45: Fox—145:
Fox—146: IWM—146-47: IWM—147: Australian War
Memorial; Robert Hunt Library—148: Flight International;
Fox—148-49: Fox—149: Fox—150-51: J. Jahr—152:
IWM—152-53: Crown Copyright—153: Crown Copyright—
154-55: IWM—156: Ministry of Defence—157: Philip Moyes;
Harry Holmes—158: P. Endsleigh Castle—159: Flight
International; Philip Moyes—160: Ministry of Defence—161:
Bruce Robertson —162: David J. Kingston—162-63: P.
Endsleigh Castle—164: Popperfoto—165: Popperfoto;
Ministry of Defence —166: IWM—166-67: Camera
Press/IWM—168: IWM —169: Fox—170: Orbis—170-71:
Keystone—171: Orbis —172: Robert Hunt Library—173:
Ullstein—174: Associated Press; Ken McDonough/Model
and Allied Publications—175: Ullstein—176: Ullstein—177:
IWM—178: Late E.L. Foot; Camera Press/IWM—178-79:
IWM— 180: Chaz Bowyer—181: Private collection; Private
collection—182: Private collection; E.G. Gee—183: Bruce
Robertson; Private collection—184-86: Public Archives of
Canada—187: G. Bingham; Bundesarchiv— 188:
Bundesarchiv—189: James Gilbert; Mike Jerram— 190-91:
James Goulding; Radio Times Hulton Picture Library—191:
Mike Jerram; Radio Times Hulton Picture Library—192:
Radio Times Hulton Picture Library; G. Bingham—193-94:
James Gilbert—194-95: J. Bingham— 195: M. Jerram—196:
M. Jerram; J. Gilbert—197: RAF Museum, Hendon; MoD,
Crown Copyright—198: RAF Museum, Hendon—199: Fox
Photos; John Frost Newspaper Collection—200: Shuttleworth
Trust; Fox Photos— 201-02: James Gilbert—203: Beagle
Aircraft; James Gilbert—204-05: MoD Crown Copyright—
205: Keystone—206: MoD Crown Copyright—207-08: James
Gilbert; Beech Aircraft—208-09: National Archives of
Canada— 209: Philip Moyes; Beech Aircraft—210-11: James
Gilbert—212-13: Beech Aircraft—214: Fox—214-15: P.
Endsleigh Castle—215: Bruce Robertson; US Air Force
—216: Bell Aerospace; Popperfoto—217: Bell Aerospace;
Flight International—219: Mike Jerram 219-20: Bell
Aerospace—220: Bruce Robertson—221: James Gilbert;
John W. Underwood Collection—222-25: John W.
Underwood Collection—226: Bellanca; John W. Underwood
Collection—227: MoD Crown Copyright; Imperial War
Museum—228-29: Philip Moyes; Shorts— 230: Shorts—231:
M.B. Passingham—232: Bruce Robertson—232-33: P.
Endsleigh Castle—233: Bruce Robertson—234: K. Brookes—
235: M.B. Passingham— 236-237: MoD Crown Copyright—
238: MoD Crown Copyright—238-39: J. Jahr—239: C.
Harrison—240: Keystone; MoD Crown Copyright.

The Illustrated Encyclopedia of
AVIATION

Marshall Cavendish New York & London

Contents

FLYING WINDMILLS

Juan de la Cierva's rotary-wing predecessor of the helicopter

Today nearly all rotary-winged aircraft are helicopters, but it is important to remember that helicopters are only one of several classes of rotary-winged aircraft. The helicopter is supported by one or more lifting rotors driven by its engine or engines. The first were built as early as 1907, but the difficulties were so great that no practical helicopter was designed for more than thirty years. Long before then the autogiro was an accomplished fact. The autogiro owed its existence to a single man, the young Spaniard Don Juan de la Cierva. He registered the name as a trade mark, but today the spelling 'autogyro' is also used for this class of flying machines.

Cierva came of rich parents and before World War I had shown his remarkable talents by rebuilding a crashed aeroplane and demonstrating that his rebuild was better than the original. By 1917 he had designed and supervised the construction of a large, multi-engined bomber-transport, by far the largest then built in Spain; but on its first flight it was crashed by an over-enthusiastic pilot more used to flying fighters. Cierva realised that the aeroplane had stalled in a violent turn near the ground. He asked himself how a heavier-than-air flying machine could be built with some kind of moving wing, arranged in such a way that it could never stall. Flapping wings were not promising (though they were virtually the only kind studied by most of the would-be aviators a hundred years earlier), and by 1920 Cierva had decided there must be a kind of horizontal propeller, with three or more wings rotating about a vertical axis. He proposed that the wings should not be driven by the engine, as in the helicopter, but rotate freely. In effect he proposed an aeroplane, with conventional engine, propeller and tail, but with the wings in the form of a rotor. He intended to suspend the fuselage from the rotor by means of a braced pylon above the centre of gravity.

Proving the concept

After making tests to see what would happen, Cierva satisfied himself that the rotary wings would, in fact, rotate. But there were severe problems of instability. Fortunately he did not become sidetracked with biplane rotors or multi-rotor configurations, and by 1923 he had built an autogiro that worked. It had blades articulated to the hub by pivots, to flap slightly up on the leading side of the rotor, where the speed of the blade through the air was the sum of the rotor speed plus the whole machine's forward speed, and flap down again on the other side, where the blade's airspeed was only the difference of these values.

Some of these early autogiros had small fixed wings and in cruising flight they were very much like aeroplanes. They were controlled by conventional stick and pedals working elevators, ailerons and rudder, and they were propelled by an ordinary propeller. The rotor was kept turning by air flowing diagonally up through the disc swept by the blades; in other words it autorotated, just like a helicopter rotor after engine failure. In contrast, a helicopter in normal powered flight puts all its engine power into the rotor system. The helicopter's main rotor is tilted slightly forward, to give both lift and propulsive thrust, and the air is driven diagonally downwards past the blades.

The Cierva C.6C, built in 1926 by Avro. It was powered by a 130 hp Clerget engine and incorporated an Avro 504 fuselage

Above: Juan de la Cierva, the inventor of the autogiro, pictured in one of his later designs. His death in an airliner crash at Croydon in 1936 signalled the end of inter-war autogiro development.
Below: an Avro-built Cierva C.19 Mark III autogiro pictured at Martlesham Heath about 1931. The C.19 was the first of the series to introduce automatic starting and the type was also manufactured by Focke in Germany. This machine was scrapped in 1932

Kinship with the helicopter

In the early Cierva machines the take-off was like an aeroplane's, with a short forward run. This got the rotor spinning and the machine could then be lifted off and climbed away quite steeply. During the 1930s Cierva made two large advances. One was the 'direct control' autogiro, with no wings and with the inclination of the rotor disc controlled directly by the pilot, via a long lever extending from the hub to the cockpit, to steer the aircraft and govern its speed. The other was the 'jump start' autogiro. This had a drive from the engine to spin up the rotor before take-off, with the blades in fine pitch. The drive was then declutched, the blade pitch increased, and the machine lifted straight upwards, thereafter climbing away and flying like other autogiros. This increased the autogiro's kinship with the helicopter, but it was still a half-way concept between the helicopter and fixed-wing aeroplane. Early types were made, often under Cierva licence, by Avro, de Havilland, Westland, Kellett, Parnall, Pitcairn, Flettner, Kayaba and several TsAGI design groups in the USSR.

Left and below: the Wallis WA-116 is an example of a modern gyrocopter. This machine was modified to accept a 60 hp Franklin engine on its return from five years of service in Sri Lanka

Sporting gyrocopters

Today most autogiros are sporting lightplanes, the biggest producer being Bensen in the United States with a range of plans, kits and complete machines of which most have a small engine with pusher propeller behind the pilot. Most of the modern small autogiros are called gyrocopters, an unfortunate extra name when a perfectly good term already existed.

No autogiro has been built in the same quantity as helicopters or aeroplanes, despite the fact that as a form of flying machine it combines features of both. One of the drawbacks of the autogiro is that it has the performance limitations of the helicopter – at least, those built so far do – while it does not offer the helicopter's big advantage in being able to hover, or fly sideways or backwards. All autogiros, gyrocopters, or gyroplanes have to maintain a forward speed high enough to keep the rotor turning. If necessary they can descend steeply with little forward speed, but this still keeps the air flowing up past the blades to keep them spinning. Thus, an autogiro could get into a very small landing area, but unless it had a temporary drive to the rotor, offering jump-start capability, it could never take off again. Another of the drawbacks of today's small machines is an extremely bad safety record, but this is due in part to factors unconnected with the concept. There is no reason why better autogiros should not be as safe as helicopters or aeroplanes.

Sinews of Czech Air Power

The Avia company made a significant contribution to Czechoslovakia's air strength between the wars

Thanks mainly to the Avia company, the young state of Czechoslovakia established both a tremendous reputation for its military aircraft and also a thriving export business between the world wars. The company built a number of civil aircraft and some foreign designs under licence, but its reputation was won with its own designs, most of which were combat aircraft.

Avia was set up in 1919 by the newly created Czech government in what had been a sugar works at Cakovice on the east side of Prague. It formed a design team led by P. Benes and M. Hajn; thus its early designs had numbers prefaced by BH. Boldly the company began with a cantilever, low-wing monoplane, the BH-1 lightplane, and developed the BH-3 fighter from this. The BH-3 was the world's most modern-looking fighter of 1921. Five were built with a 185hp BMW IIIa engine, reaching 214km/h (133mph), followed by five with the Czech Walter W-IV of 220hp, which raised the speed to 225km/h (140mph). They were followed by a truly outstanding biplane fighter, the BH-21 of 1924, powered by the 300hp Skoda (Hispano licence) HS 8Fb engine. About 120 were built for the Czech Army Air Force, and 50 more were made for the Belgian Air Force by the SABCA company under licence. Speed with two Vickers 7·7mm guns was 240km/h (150mph), and a special racing version won the Czech 1925 national air races at over 300km/h (186·7mph).

Licence-built Fokkers

In the mid-1920s Czech civil aviation began to emerge from its early doldrums and though the first scheduled airline, CSA, used equipment from other manufacturers, Avia itself operated the parcel route between Prague and Liberec using its BH-11 lightplane. On 2 May 1927 the second airline, CLS, began its mainly-domestic operations using a fleet of six Avia BH-25s. These were comfortable wooden biplanes, carrying six passengers and they were powered by the 420hp Walter-built Jupiter engine. But when CLS bought the widely-used Fokker F.VIIb-3m in 1928, it was clear that this Dutch airliner was an excellent design and Avia bought a manufacturing licence. At least eight were built for CLS and five for CSA in 1930, while further machines were built for the Czech Army Air Force and other customers, using five types of engine including Avia's own DR 14. The company also built larger tri-

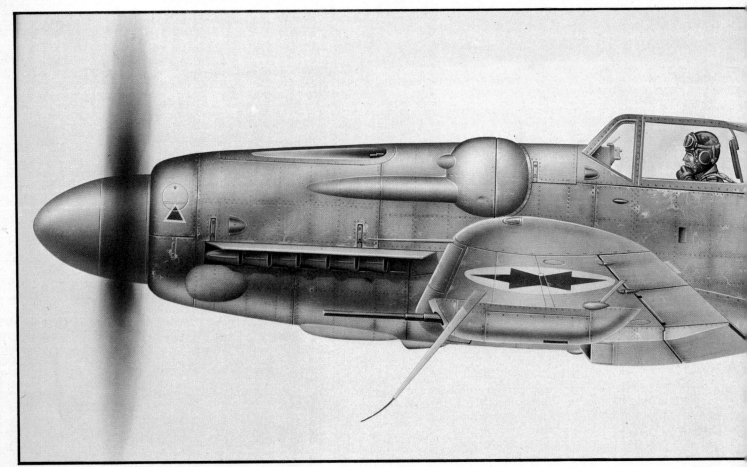

nearly all were powered by the Walter-built Jupiter. It was the first Avia fighter to have a fin, and in its original form went into licence-production at the Polish PWS works in 1928. In 1929 the redesigned BH-33E appeared, with steel-tube fuselage, new top wing and other changes, and this flew so well at the 1929 Paris Salon that it was sold to the USSR and built under licence by Ikarus in Jugoslavia. Re-engined with the 525 hp Skoda L water-cooled vee-12 it went into production at Avia as the BH-33L, adopted as the Ba 33 for the Czech Army Air Force. Armament was two fixed Vickers guns, firing Czech 7·9 mm ammunition, and the maximum speed was 296 km/h.

Nowotny soon set to work improving this model, and in 1931 his B 34 appeared, with duralumin panels over a steel-tube fuselage and 850 hp Avia Vr-36 vee-12 engine. In 1932 this was flown with several other engines and, by August 1933, had been refined into the B 534 with 860 hp Hispano-Suiza 12Ydrs engine made by Avia under licence. Armed with four Mk 30 machine guns (originally two were in the lower wing, but production aircraft had a pair on each side of the fuselage), the B 534 was a small and extremely formidable machine, capable of 375 km/h (233 mph). Later versions had an enclosed cockpit and some had spats, up-rated engines or 20 mm Hispano cannon firing through the propeller hub. In September 1938 over 300 had been delivered, so when Hitler marched into Czechoslovakia the Czech Army Air Force was stronger in fighters than the Luftwaffe. Eventually 445 were built, most serving on the Russian front from June 1941; many Avia pilots deserted to the Soviet Union and three B 534-IV fighters fought against the Germans in the 1944 Slovak revolt.

The German occupation

As a result of a 1935 pact with the Soviet Union, the Czech Army Air Force adopted the outstanding Tupolev SB-2

motor aircraft based on the Fokker F.IX, initially because of the need for a heavy bomber. The first batch of 12 F.IX bombers were built in 1932. They were powered by 450 hp Walter Jupiters, had a variety of arrangements of upper and lower defensive guns and carried bomb-loads of either 800 or 1500 kg (1,763 or 3,306 lb). The F.39 was Avia's own civil development, built as a 17-seat airliner and for government VIP use, and usually powered by the 640 hp Walter Pegasus II with ring cowling.

Classic fighters

In 1930 Avia appointed a new chief designer, Frantiszek Nowotny, the firm having become a subsidiary of the great Skoda arms group. Benes and Hajn left to join CKD-Praga, but they left behind the standard fighter of the Czech Army Air Force, the BH-33. First flown in 1927, it was a radial-engined development of the BH-21 and

Above right: an Avia BH-3 of 1921. One of the most advanced warplanes of its day, it was both fast and highly manoeuvrable. Below: an Avia S199 of the Israeli air force. This intractable derivative of the Messerschmitt Bf109 was nicknamed Mezek (Mule) by its Czech pilots

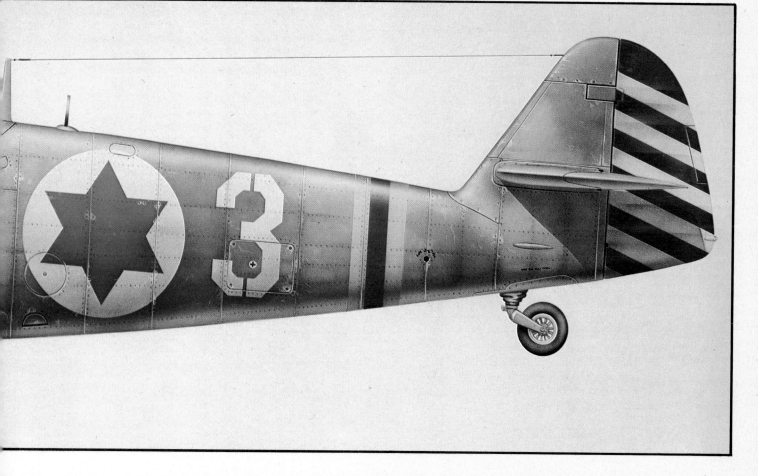

as its standard medium bomber and, as well as buying 54, ordered large numbers from its home industry. Avia tooled up in 1938 to build 66 and to develop it as the Avia B 71 Czech bomber, but the programme was halted by the German occupation. Likewise the Germans temporarily halted Nowotny's promising monoplane fighter, the B 35, which flew at the time of the Munich crisis in September 1938. The original Av-135 had been intended to have a 1,000 hp Avia-built Hispano 12Y engine and retractable landing gear, but the prototype, designated Av-35-1, had only 860 hp and a fixed gear with spats. Eventually the Germans let the programme continue, and the outcome was a run of 12 Av-135 fighters for Bulgaria in 1941. These did have retractable landing gear, but only 890 hp from an Avia-built Hispano Ycrs, giving a maximum speed of 534 km/h (332 mph). The wing had a straight leading-edge

Top: a line-up of Avia B 534 fighters. This type formed the backbone of the Czech fighter force between 1934 and 1939 and 445 of them were built.
Above: the BH-21 of the 1920s was another outstanding fighter aircraft. It was especially noted as an aerobatic aeroplane.
Left: one of twelve Fokker F. IX bombers, licence-built by Avia for the Czech air force.
Below: the German occupation of Czechoslovakia halted development of the B 35 monoplane fighter, but 12 improved B 135s were built for Bulgaria in 1941

and curved trailing-edge, and armament comprised one 20 mm cannon and two synchronised machine guns.

Avia's last aircraft, before its reorganisation into the State Automobile and Aircraft Organization in 1947, stemmed from the use of Czech industry as a source of German arms during World War II. The Messerschmitt Bf 109G had been assembled at Prague-Cakovice from parts made at dispersed manufacturing units throughout Czechoslovakia. In 1945 Avia engineers managed to collect 500 sets of usable Bf 109G airframe parts and equipment, and set up a production line. Only 20 could be built as Avia S 99 fighters, with the DB 605AM engine; the rest had to be completed as the S 199 with Jumo 211F (ex-Ju 88) turning a broad-bladed, slow-speed propeller. The resulting malicious fighter was called Mezek (Mule) for obvious reasons.

Warplanes for the Central Powers

The Aviatik companies produced military aeroplanes for both Germany and Austria-Hungary in World War I

Aircraft with the family name Aviatik were important combat types of the Central Powers in the First World War. All were products of either the Automobil und Aviatik AG of Germany, or its Austro-Hungarian subsidiary the Oesterreichische-Ungarische Flugzeugfabrik Aviatik (OUFA) of Vienna. Aviatiks were built in each of the three main categories of combat aeroplanes used by the Central Powers: B, for reconnaissance (usually without armament); C, two-seaters with front and rear armament; and D, single-seat fighters.

Before August 1914 the German company's main works had been at Mülhausen (Mulhouse) in Alsace. This region (which again became part of France after the war) was rightly judged vulnerable and soon after the start of hostilities the company headquarters was moved to Freiburg-im-Breisgau in eastern Germany. Here work began on the B.I two-seater, which was intended for reconnaissance duties with the Imperial German Army Aviation Service. Powered by a 100 hp Mercedes D.I, of the water-cooled, six-cylinder, in-line form that became almost universal for German and Austro-Hungarian aero engines in World War I, it proved to be a sound and completely satisfactory machine and was in service on the Western Front in a matter of weeks.

Production in Austria-Hungary

In 1915 the same basic design was adopted by the Austro-Hungarian company as the Austrian Aviatik B.II. This had a 120 hp Austro-Daimler and could at once be distinguished by the different shape of its rudder and elevators with horn balances which overhung the fixed surfaces. Bomb racks were added for a pair of 10 kg (22 lb) bombs, but the only guns carried were small arms taken aboard by the crew. The observer sat in the front cockpit and had a fair view downwards ahead of the wing. The pilot sat behind, and his view was rather poor. These machines, called Series 32, were extremely slow, only just being able to exceed 100 km/h (63 mph); on the other hand they were easy to fly and reliable, and their endurance of 4 hr was often found to be very useful.

By mid-1915 the Series 32 had been superseded in production by the Series 33, the Aviatik B.III. Two improvements were the substitution of the 160 hp version of the Austro-Daimler engine for the 120 hp engine of the Series 32 and the transposition of pilot and observer. The pilot sat in the front of the Series 33's single large cockpit, which allowed the crew to communicate easily and even change places. The observer had a cumbrous 7·92 mm Schwarzlose army machine gun on a pillar mount with a good field of

A captured Aviatik C.I. The type first appeared in 1915 and carried the observer in the front cockpit. Note the rail at the side of the cockpit on which the Parabellum gun could be mounted.

fire to the rear. Unfortunately, to carry the extra weight the wings were increased in span and, to counter the rearward shift of centre of gravity caused by the machine gun, the wingtips were raked back. This made the B.III extremely sluggish to control and in gusty conditions it became almost unmanageable, earning the nicknames 'rocking chair' and 'gondola'. For this reason the next production batch, Series 34, reverted to the B.II airframe, but had the engine and cockpit of the B.III. It was appreciably better to handle and had much higher performance, even though it could carry three 20 kg (44 lb) bombs against the three 10 kg (22 lb) of the B.III. During 1916 the Aviatik B-series aircraft were progressively transferred to second-line duties as trainers, having outlived their usefulness as combat machines at the front.

Armed two-seaters

The Aviatik C.I bore strong resemblance to the Austrian B-series when it appeared in 1915 and it was made in a similar way with airframe predominantly of wood and covered with fabric, except for duralumin panels over the front of the fuselage. Though it had the 160 hp Mercedes D.III engine, the C.I put the pilot in the rear, while the observer in the front cockpit could mount his Parabellum machine gun on a rail on either side of the engine cowl. This gave an unsatisfactory field of fire, because the gun could not reasonably be swapped over from one side to the other in combat. In any case the crew disposition was inconvenient, giving the pilot a poor view and leaving the aircraft unprotected from the rear. The result was the same as in the B-series, and the rearranged C.Ia with observer in the rear, with his gun on a Schneider ring mount, went into production in late 1915 at Aviatik and at the Hannoversche Wagonfabrik. Small batches were also built of the C.II with 200 hp Benz Bz.IV. The final Aviatik C model was the C.III of 1916, which was merely a cleaned up and streamlined C.Ia with the same 160 hp engine. Though it was a little over 100 kg heavier, at 1337 kg (2,948 lb), it was

Above left: the first production Austrian Aviatik B.II of 1915. Note the red and white stripes on the flying surfaces and fuselage, which were national markings. Below: the popular and reliable Aviatik C.III which had a top speed of 100 mph

considerably faster, being able to reach 161 km/h (100 mph) compared with only 143 km/h for the C.II. Though a few were built with the back-to-front crew arrangement, most C.IIIs were popular and reliable machines and most carried twin Parabellum guns, which made them prickly customers.

The Aviatik D.I was Austro-Hungary's first and most important single-seat fighter. It was started under the direction of the OUFA's chief designer, Julius von Berg, as soon as the B-series had been completed, and the type was commonly called the Berg D.I, or Berg Scout. Apart from the struts and the tail unit, the construction was wooden, with ply-covered fuselage. The latter was tall and deep, and the pilot was perched in line with the trailing edge where he could see above as well as below the top wing. The rather stubby, fabric-covered wings had marked washout (reduced incidence toward the tips), only the upper plane having ailerons. The wings were rather thin and contemporary accounts state that several wings failed catastrophically during flight manoeuvres. Another shortcoming was overheating of the Austro-Daimler engine and there are photographs showing 'Berg Scouts' in flight with the cowling top panels, and even side panels, left off to help the water cooling system.

The prototype, designated Series 30.16, appeared in early 1916, followed by a machine closer to the final form in 1917, with the designation 30.21. Production Aviatik D.Is followed in the summer of 1917, at least 700 being delivered by Aviatik (Series 38, 138, 238 and 338) Thöne und Fiala (101), Lohner (115), M.A.G. (92) and W.K.F. (84, 184, 284 and 384). Early batches had engines of 185 hp or 225 hp, but the standard Austro-Daimler was rated at 200 hp or 210 hp, giving this nippy-looking fighter a speed of 185 km/h (115 mph). There seems to have been some difficulty in the armament installation. Early machines had a single 7·92 mm Schwarzlose mounted on the upper wing, but nearly all had twin synchronised guns–installed so far forward, alongside the engine cylinders, that the pilot could not reach the breeches to clear a stoppage. In service the D.I's performance was adequate, though some of the most influential pilots in the Austro-Hungarian Jagdkompanien preferred the locally built Albatros or even the Hansa-Brandenburg D.I.

Top: the prototype of the Austrian Aviatik triplane fighter, which was not produced.
Above: a long-range version of the Berg Scout for photographic reconnaissance duties, which carried a camera inside the fuselage.
Above left: the 40th Austrian Aviatik produced, powered by a 185 hp Austro-Daimler engine, with armament of one Schwarzlose machine gun

A.V. Roe's Old Stager

The Avro 504 was one of the earliest bombers of World War I and was still in service as a trainer in the 1930s

Squadron Commander Arthur Bigsworth in front of one of the RNAS Avro 504Bs which tried to intercept the Zeppelin LZ.39 over Ostend on 17 May 1915. The 504C interceptor version was developed as a result of this incident

Until recently the legendary Avro 504 held the record as the military aircraft that remained both in production and in service longest. Today its record has been eclipsed, but that in no way detracts from its amazing achievement. No other aeroplane flying in 1913 was in production in 1933 and the fact that during these twenty years the 504 was developed to its full potential is yet a further tribute to the excellence of the basic design.

In view of this unique record it may seem surprising to record that Alliott Verdon-Roe – who used a shortened version of his name (Avro) for his company – thought he would be lucky to get an order for six 504s at the start of the type's career. In 1913 military aircraft were officially the prerogative of the Royal Aircraft Factory and A. V. Roe, as an outsider, had the dice loaded against him. There was at that time little concept of specialized fighter or bomber types. The objective was just to build safe and reliable aeroplanes, whose main functions were regarded as training and reconnaissance. The Avro Type E, with the constructor's type number 500, had already been ordered by the Royal Flying Corps early in 1913. It was a two-bay biplane with two seats in tandem. In June the first 504

appeared, flying at Brooklands the following month powered by an 80 hp Gnome rotary. It closely resembled the 500, but had an even better performance and in the winter 1913–14, after minor modifications, it set a British height record at 4395 m (14,420 ft) and also recorded the excellent speed of 130·2 km/h (80·9 mph).

Reconnaissance and bombing

This original 504 model was probably the most satisfactory all-round aeroplane in the world at the time, because it lacked nothing in sweet handling, robustness or reliability. The RFC ordered twelve and the Royal Naval Air Service one, and these orders were later increased to 63. Deliveries were rapid, and these completely undeveloped but extremely useful machines were exceedingly busy throughout the early months of the war. Though the RFC aircraft were assigned to reconnaissance duties, Avro No. 383 was armed as early as mid-October 1914 by fitting a Lewis gun for the observer in the rear cockpit, the instigator of this experiment being 2nd Lt L. A. Strange of 5 Sqn.

The early RNAS Avros were pressed into service as strategic bombers. Some carried four 7 kg (16 lb) or 9 kg

intercept LZ.39 over the Ostend area. These encounters prompted the RNAS to order a special interceptor 504. By 1915 the 504A and B were in quantity production, mainly as trainers—the type having survived a confrontation with officialdom, which proposed dropping the type in favour of the 'Factory'-built B.E.2c. The RFC's 504A had short-span ailerons, while the RNAS 504B had standard ailerons and introduced a fixed fin. All early RNAS machines had cut-outs of distinctive shape at the trailing edge roots of the lower planes, Admiralty-size spars and, usually, cockpits that cut the upper fuselage longerons. All 504s at this time had a skid projecting ahead of the landing gear to protect the propeller and prevent nose-overs on soft ground.

This RNAS 504B model served as the basis for 80

(20lb) Harris bombs on external racks, while on short missions the front cockpit was occupied by the observer with a Lewis gun for ground strafing. The most celebrated mission of these aircraft took place on 21 November 1914. Four Avros set out from Belfort loaded with Harris bombs, and three made the 402 km (250 miles) flight to the Zeppelin works at Friedrichshafen. One of the three was shot down and the pilot captured, but against this a Zeppelin was destroyed, a gasworks put out of action, the Zeppelin factory damaged and a tremendous impression made on friend and foe alike. These flimsy 80 hp Avros are generally held to have made the world's first long-range aerial attack. It could not be repeated, because of the advance of the German armies.

Zeppelin interceptors

The RNAS also used their early 504s to intercept Zeppelins, but they did not have an adequate margin of speed and climb for this role. On 17 May 1915 Flt-Sub-Lt R. H. Mulock at last got within firing distance of LZ.38 over Essex, but his Lewis gun jammed as he tried long-range firing. On the same night several RNAS Avros tried to

Avro 504C single-seat interceptors, of which 50 were built by Brush Electrical of Loughborough. The 504C had an additional petrol tank in what had been the front (observer's) cockpit and a normal armament of one Lewis ·303 in machine gun firing over the upper centre-section. The 504C entered service in June 1915 as Britain's standard home-defence night fighter. At that time the RNAS bore the responsibility for UK defence against air attack and these Avros were stationed at nearly all the RNAS eastern airfields, with main units at Dover, Westgate, Eastchurch, Hendon, Chingford, Felixstowe, Great Yarmouth, Cranwell, Redcar and East Fortune, with a further Home Defence unit in France at RNAS Dunkirk.

The Mono-Avro

Unusual 504 fighters included a single-seat 504B conversion used by the RNAS in the Aegean and the 504F powered by the 75 hp water-cooled Rolls-Royce Hawk (usually an RNAS airship engine). The 504D was a single-seat version used in small numbers by the RFC in 1915.

Later in 1915 the first 'Mono-Avro' appeared, fitted

Top: an Avro 504J of the School of Special Flying, Gosport, where they were standard equipment for pilot training in the last two years of World War I. Above: an Avro 504K built by the Eastbourne Aviation company. The 504K was the most numerous of the wartime marks, many earlier versions being updated

with the 100 hp Gnome Monosoupape engine. This was the 504E, an RNAS two-seater with the rear cockpit moved further back and other changes, including less stagger between the wings. The 504G was an RNAS two-seater with a Scarff-ring Lewis in the rear cockpit and synchronised Vickers fired by the pilot, who now sat in front. Its purpose was gunnery training. The 504H was the first aircraft strengthened for catapulting for shipboard use.

The greatest production in 1916 was of the 504J trainer, the famous type around which R. R. Smith-Barry planned the world's first proper system of flying training at Gosport. This Avro was the best-known Mono-Avro and over 30,000 pilots were trained on it and the 504K before the Armistice. It was basically an RFC machine, with short ailerons and balanced rudder, and was built by a number of contractors – the final list of British companies building the 504 numbering sixteen. By 1917 the variety of engines available and increasing shortage of the Monosoupape caused Avro, by now a major company, to produce the 504K in which an open-fronted cowl and special engine bearers allowed almost any rotary to be installed. Engines fitted included the Mono, the 110 hp Le Rhône or the 130 hp Clerget. About three-quarters of the total British wartime output of 504s (a total of 8,340) were either Ks, or early A and J models brought approximately to K standard.

In early 1918 the increasing attentions of large, high-flying Zeppelins led to a further anti-Zeppelin 504 variant: the night-fighter 504K. The front cockpit was faired over, a windmill electric generator was fitted and the cylindrical petrol tank on the upper centre-section was moved across to make room for a Lewis on a Foster mounting, with a Hutton illuminated night-firing sight. These machines could climb to about 3000 m (10,000 ft) in 15 minutes and reach a speed at that height of about 137 km/h (85 mph).

Most 504s had the excellent endurance of eight hours and some of the single-seaters with extra tanks could patrol even longer. On the other hand the ceiling of around 5500 m (18,000 ft) was not high enough to enable the largest Zeppelins to be intercepted and, though five RAF Home Defence squadrons were still equipped with the 504K single-seater at the Armistice, it was planned to replace them with Sopwith Camels.

By the Armistice in November 1918, a few 504L float-seaplanes had been built and a very small number of various sub-types had been built in Canada. Remarkably, apart from 52 sold to the American Expeditionary Force in July 1918, all the vast output of Avros had been used by the RFC, RNAS and RAF. It was beyond question the

Above and opposite top:
An Avro 504K preserved
by the Shuttleworth Trust,
which was converted from a
Lynx-engined 504N.
Opposite bottom: A
night-fighter 504 prepares
for take-off.
Below: The Avro 504K
flown by F. P. Raynham
in the 1923 Grosvenor
Trophy pictured before the
race at Lympne

most important single trainer of the Allies, and one of the more significant and useful operational machines.

After 1918 the 504K continued as a leading type with the RAF, while hundreds of 504s were dispersed to other countries. Many were used for civil purposes, while Avro developed a wealth of civil and military descendents which saw only limited production. In the Soviet Union, however, the 504 became one of the first standard types. After the years of revolutionary fighting there were few aircraft and no surviving aircraft industry and the 504's qualities were well-suited to local conditions. Details are sparse, but the Soviet U-1 version, basically an Avro 504K powered by a locally-built Le Rhône, was certainly built in more than one factory over a period of some six years and the number produced was at least 1,000 and probably well over 3,000.

The final variant

The final 504 variant emerged during the mid-1920s after various engines had been flown in 504Ks and prototypes of the new model. The 504N took some time to evolve, but it was finally adopted in 1926 as the RAF's first post-war design of trainer. The engine chosen was the Armstrong Siddeley Lynx static radial, of 160hp, 180hp, or 215hp–the 504N thus often being called the Lynx-Avro. It was a cleaner and more modern-looking machine than the 504K which it replaced. The landing gear had oleo-pneumatic shock absorbers and no skid. The old RFC-type balanced rudder, with no fin, was retained, but the fuselage

Right: a civil-registered Avro 504N takes off from Croydon during the King's Cup air race of 1925. Right bottom: the Central Flying School established the world's first instrument flying course. Note the collapsible hood on the rear cockpit of this 504N of 'E' Flight, CFS

During World War I a total of 8,340 Avro 504s were built; 3,696 of them by the parent company and the remainder by fifteen other manufacturers in Britain. The type served mainly with training units, but Avro 504s were also used in France, the Middle East and for Home Defence. The American Expeditionary Force bought the type in 1918.

was made less box-like by two additional stringers along the sides. Fuel was carried in twin tanks faired under the upper wing on each side and the engine was uncowled. Production of new 504Ns began in 1927 and a total of 570 had been delivered when the production line finally closed in 1933. A few were conversions of earlier 504K models and a few foreign 504Ks were rebuilt to N standard. The 504N served as the standard basic trainer with the Central Flying School and all five of the RAF Flying Training Schools, as well as with the Auxiliary Air Force and University Air Squadrons. Early examples had traditional wooden airframes and distinctive tapered ailerons, which completely altered the appearance of the aircraft, but most of the newly built 504Ns had different airframes with a welded, steel-tube fuselage and untapered ailerons of the Frise type.

Under the hood

One of the many achievements of the 504N was the establishment of the art of instrument flying in the RAF. Six aircraft of the Central Flying School's 'E' Flight operated the first-ever course in blind flying anywhere in the world in September 1931. The technique had been developed by such pioneers as W. E. P. Johnson from 1929, entirely in 504Ns of the CFS, using the recently perfected Reid & Sigrist turn/slip indicator and later the artificial horizon. This work was quite independent of American pioneering

by Elmer Sperry, Kollsman and Jimmy Doolittle and it put the RAF ahead in the new technique of teaching pupils to fly 'under the hood' with no vision outside the cockpit. These 504s had one degree less dihedral than usual, to reduce inherent lateral stability and thus make the pilot fly the aircraft positively all the time.

Other duties of the 504N included crazy flying in the humorous 'pupil and instructor' act at the annual RAF Display at Hendon. When they were progressively replaced by their family successor, the larger Avro Tutor, from 1933, large numbers of 504Ns came on to the civil market–just as the 504J and K had done in 1919. Both with the Lynx and re-engined with the Mongoose, these aircraft passed their twilight years giving thousands of British people their first brief 'joy ride'.

Above: a shortage of Monosoupape engines led to the Avro 504K being equipped with a variety of engines, this example being powered by a 110hp Le Rhône rotary

Faithful Annie

The dependable and versatile Anson served in many combat and training roles

Below: the Anson was one of the most important aeroplanes supplied to Canada under the British Commonwealth Air Training Plan (a Mk 1 is shown).
Bottom: the Canadians built their own versions of the Anson, including the Mk V pictured

'Faithful Annie' was the nickname bestowed upon the Avro Anson, and, as all who knew the aeroplane would agree, it was highly appropriate. Not only was 'Annie' utterly reliable, but she also outlived her great ancestor the Avro 504 of 1913 and was even more widely used. This 'lady-of-all-work' was in continuous production for seventeen years and nearly 11,000 were built. Her rather quaint figure underwent changes from time to time, but never to such an extent that she was not immediately recognisable. She always had the stamp of a thorough-bred, and her pilots and aircrew held her in high esteem – despite such little snags, on some models, as fuel cock controls that were rather tricky in an emergency and man-ual undercarriage retraction that seemed like winding-up a pail of water from an 80-foot well.

Nice to handle – pilots said 'She flies herself' – 'Annie' gave long and unfailing service in peace and war, being used for such diverse tasks as coastal reconnaissance, crew training, passenger transport, survey, crop dusting, freight carrying and ambulance duties. The RAF used her for no less than thirty-two years (1936–1968) and during World War II she was one of the mainstays of the vast British Commonwealth Air Training Plan in Canada,

Australia and New Zealand. Pilots in almost every branch of civil and military flying came to know her, but today 'Annie' is well-nigh extinct. However, as befits a truly classic aeroplane, a few examples have somehow been spared the unworthy fate of the breaker's yard and are thus still with us, albeit, in most cases, as non-flying relics.

The Anson was designed by Roy Chadwick (who later designed the Lancaster) and his team and was derived from the Avro Type 652 six-passenger civil transport, two of which were delivered to Imperial Airways in March 1935 and used for several years on the long Croydon-Brindisi route. Work on the Type 652A, as the Anson was designated, began a year earlier, on 7 May 1934, when the Air Ministry notified Avro that it wished to consider possible designs for a twin-engined landplane for coastal reconnaissance duties. The required disposable load matched that of the Type 652 as then designed almost exactly and, furthermore, the invitation to tender asked for 'details of the extent to which any of your existing types can be adapted to meet the requirements'. On 19 May the Avro 652A design was offered and in the follow-ing September the Air Ministry chose it and a conversion of the de Havilland DH89 Dragon Rapide from fifteen competitive designs submitted by the aircraft industry and ordered one prototype of each. Avro was given just six months to design and build the 652A at a time when the first 652 (G-ACRM *Avalon*) was itself far from complete.

Coastal reconnaissance
Nevertheless, on 7 January 1935 flight trials began with this new civil transport – the first low-wing monoplane

with the bomb release, was operated by the navigator/ bomb aimer from a prone position, although the pilot also had a bomb release. The bomb load totalled 164kg (360lb), usually made up of two 45kg (100lb) anti-submarine bombs and several smaller bombs, smoke floats, or flares, and was stowed in the centre-section. When not bomb aiming, the navigator sat at a chart table midway between the pilot and the big parrot-cage-style Armstrong Whitworth dorsal turret. There was also a spare seat alongside the pilot which he could use.

On 6 March 1936 the Anson began to enter service with No. 48 Squadron at Manston, Kent, thereby becoming the first monoplane to reach the squadrons under the RAF Expansion Scheme and also the first to have a retractable undercarriage. That same year Avro announced in one of its foreign sales brochures that, in addition to the initial RAF order for 174 Ansons, they had received orders from Australia, Egypt, Finland, Greece and Eire.

From an early stage in the Anson's history, an advanced trainer version was envisaged and several aircraft, both with and without dual controls and turrets, were supplied to various flying training units in 1937–38. The first orders for Mk I trainers were placed in 1937 and deliveries of these purpose-built aircraft began early in 1939 to Service Flying Training Schools, Elementary and Reserve Flying Training Schools and many other specialist training units. Several bomber squadrons formed under the RAF Expansion Scheme received Ansons as interim equipment, pending the availability of modern monoplane bombers such as the Handley Page Hampden and Armstrong Whitworth Whitley, and during World War II some Anson Is were fitted with Bristol power-operated gun turrets for use by Air Gunnery Schools.

Commonwealth air training

On 18 December 1939 the British Commonwealth Air Training Plan was launched and the Anson was chosen as one of its mainstays. This resulted in huge quantities of Ansons being ordered, many of which were destined to be built at Avro's new underground shadow factory at Yeadon, near Leeds. It also resulted in the Anson becoming known to tens of thousands of pilots in the United Kingdom, the Dominions and the Colonies, including men from the Allied nations. A steady increase in production took place until in 1943–44 the output reached a peak of 130 aircraft a month.

Several new versions of the Anson appeared as the war progressed, many of them converted from British-built airframes or entirely constructed in Canada. The versions evolved in Canada were the Mks III and IV with Avro-built airframes and American Jacobs or Wright engines respectively (the Mk III being eventually modified to incorporate an hydraulically-operated undercarriage and flaps); the Canadian-built and Jacobs-powered Anson II first flown in August 1941 (later modified to incorporate a moulded plywood nose, together with hydraulic undercarriage and flaps operation, and adopted by the US Army Air Corps as a crew trainer designated AT-20); and, finally, the Canadian-built Mks V and VI with American Pratt & Whitney engines, used respectively for navigational training (no turret) and armament training (Bristol power-operated turret). In order to conserve strategic materials, the fuselages of these last two marks were constructed entirely of moulded plywood.

Meanwhile, in England the Anson X appeared, with no turret and a strengthened floor, for passenger and freight carrying. The Anson, in this and other forms, was the principal taxi aircraft of the Air Transport Auxiliary,

Avro had ever built and its first to have a retractable undercarriage – and on 24 March the 652A prototype (K4771) followed it into the air, piloted by S. A. 'Bill' Thorn. Official RAF trials at the Aeroplane and Armament Experimental Establishment at Martlesham Heath, Suffolk, quickly followed and, after necessary modifications had been made to the 652A's horizontal tail surfaces, it went, together with the DH89M, for evaluation trials at the Coast Defence Development Unit at Gosport, Hants.

Soon after the Gosport trials, the 652A was able to demonstrate its superiority in range and endurance over its biplane rival during a fleet exercise off the East Coast and on 24 May 1935 the Air Ministry decided to order it in quantity. Specification 18/35 was written round K4771 in August, listing 38 special requirements for the production aircraft – which was duly named Anson, after Admiral George Anson, the famous British seaman of the eighteenth century.

The first production Anson I (K6152) made its first flight on 31 December 1935 piloted by Geoffrey Tyson. It had more powerful engines than K4771 (two 350hp Armstrong Siddeley Cheetah IXs instead of 295hp Cheetah VIs) and the most noticeable external difference was the higher, continuous line of cabin windows giving almost uninterrupted all-round vision. A crew of three was normally carried (pilot, navigator/bomb aimer, and wireless operator/air gunner), their seats being so placed that a free passage was left down the starboard side of the fuselage for movement from one part of the aircraft to another. The bomb sight was in the extreme nose and,

Although primarily a training aeroplane, the Anson was also used as a taxi aircraft for ferry pilots

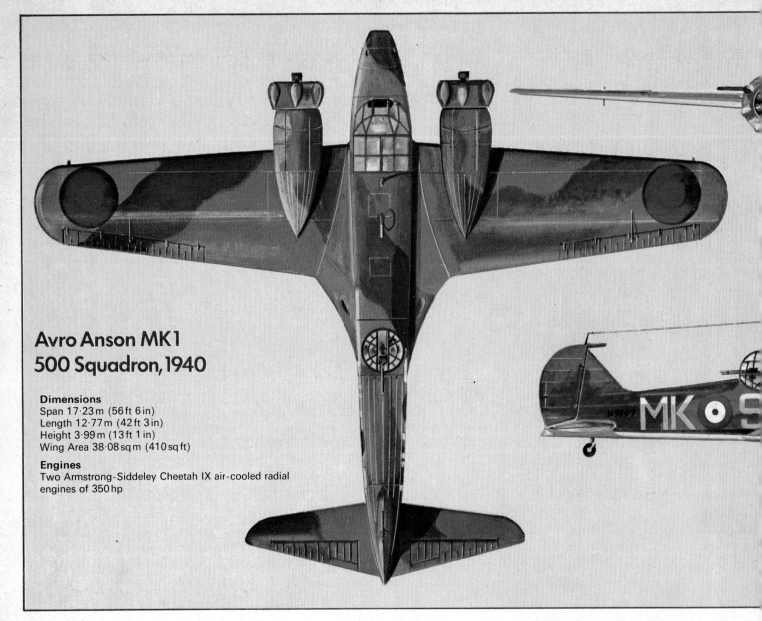

Avro Anson MK1
500 Squadron, 1940

Dimensions
Span 17·23 m (56 ft 6 in)
Length 12·77 m (42 ft 3 in)
Height 3·99 m (13 ft 1 in)
Wing Area 38·08 sq m (410 sq ft)

Engines
Two Armstrong-Siddeley Cheetah IX air-cooled radial
engines of 350 hp

Opposite: an Anson fitted with a Bristol Type 1 Mk IV turret, which was used as a gunnery trainer. Nine air gunners schools in the United Kingdom were equipped with Ansons of this type

the civilian organisation which took over the task of ferrying RAF and Royal Navy aircraft from the manufacturers to the services during World War II. Ansons logged nearly 16 million kilometres (ten million miles) in ATA service, with only eight fatalities–an accident rate so low as to be comparable with well-organised commercial airline operation. One ATA pilot described the Anson as being 'the easiest aircraft to fly that you could wish for' and another recalled that at least once in 1940 he flew in an Anson with thirteen other ferry pilots and their parachutes.

In September 1944 ATA Ansons began the emergency task of delivering urgently needed supplies, ranging from radio transmitters and receivers to mortar bombs and blood plasma, to the Second Army in Belgium. The stores were packed mostly in wooden boxes which were stowed on the cabin floor between the main wing spars, and sometimes there were so many of them that the pilot was forced to get to his seat via the port side sliding cockpit window.

Further development of the Anson led to the Marks XI and XII, both of which featured a deeper cabin with revised glazing and hydraulically-operated undercarriage and flaps (the last two items had also been incorporated in the Mk X Series II). Both marks began to replace some of the ageing Mk Is on communications duties during 1944; some were fitted out as ambulances, while others were furnished for use by various Air Attachés throughout the

world. Early 1945 saw the appearance of the Mk XIX civil feeder liner/Service communications Anson with a completely redesigned interior and windows. It was built in two main versions, with either wooden or metal wings and tailplane. Most of the latter version joined the RAF where some remained in use until as late as June 1968, when they became the last RAF Ansons to be withdrawn.

Final Anson variants were the Mks XVIII and XVIIIC, which were respectively general-purpose aircraft for the Royal Afghan Air Force and civil aircrew trainers for the Indian Government; the Mk XX bombing and navigational trainer for RAF use in Southern Rhodesia; and the Mks XXI and XXII, respectively navigational and radio trainers for RAF use at home.

Altogether, 10,996 Ansons were built (*not* 11,020 as is sometimes stated), 8,113 by Avro and 2,883 in Canada by Federal Aircraft Limited, a company formed specially for the manufacture of the type. The last Anson to be built was a Mk XXI serialled WJ661; it was officially handed over to the RAF at Avro's Woodford, Cheshire, facility on 27 May 1952.

Testing airborne radar

In 1937 an Anson was used for flight trials of the first British airborne radar to incorporate its own transmitter–a small experimental set, working on a wavelength of 240

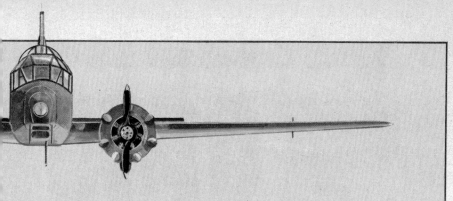

Performance
Maximum speed 300 km/h (188 mph) at 2100 m (7,000 ft)
Cruising speed 250 km/h (158 mph) at 1800 m (6,000 ft)
Service ceiling 5900 m (19,500 ft)

Armament
One fixed, forward-firing Browning 0·303 m/g and
one Vickers K 0·303 m/g in a manually operated turret

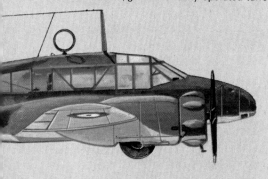

megacycles, built by Dr Edward Bowen and his team in their laboratory at Bawdsey Manor in Suffolk. The trials began in July and it was not long before large ships were being detected at ranges of up to 8 km (5 miles). On 3 September Bowen managed to locate the battleship *Rodney*, the aircraft carrier *Courageous* and the cruiser *Southampton*, which he had known when he took off to be exercising somewhere off the Suffolk coast. Next day he again took off in the Anson, bent on repeating the performance. But this time the weather began to deteriorate and the Coastal Command aircraft in the exercise were recalled by radio. Bowen's radar-equipped Anson did not pick up the recall signal, however, and continued its reconnaissance under the murkiest circumstances, finally locating some of the warships on its radar screen at a range of about 14 km (nine miles). In order to confirm the identity of the warships, the pilot closed in to within visual range and *Courageous*, believing an attack to be imminent, despatched some of her fighters to intercept. As they took off, these too duly appeared as 'blips' on the Anson's radar screen. On the return flight, through solid cloud cover up to 3650 m (12,000 ft), Bowen used the radar to help the pilot make an accurate landfall and it is recorded how that evening a surprised Duty Air Staff Officer, who had been led to believe that all flying had been cancelled, received an accurate plot of the fleet's position.

By the outbreak of World War II the Anson was already obsolescent as a combat aircraft and a much more effective weapon, in the shape of the American Lockheed Hudson, had begun to replace it in Coastal Command. Even so, all but one of the eleven general reconnaissance landplane squadrons in existence were still flying Ansons and they were immediately employed on reconnaissance over the North Sea and the Channel, convoy escort duties and anti-submarine patrols.

Despite their obsolescence, Ansons could, and did, give a good account of themselves in aerial combat. On 8 November 1939, for instance, an Anson fought two Dornier Do 18 flying boats, forcing one into the sea. Another Anson on patrol encountered an enemy aircraft, fired the moment the pilot saw the black crosses on its

wings, and with the first burst sent it straight into the sea, where it broke up and sank before its type could be identified.

Combat experience

Standard defensive armament of the Anson I was a single moveable machine-gun in the dorsal turret and a fixed forward firing machine-gun in the port side of the nose. However, as a result of combat experience, Anson squadrons beefed-up this fire power by improvising machine-gun mountings in the cabin, with the guns firing through the windows to cover the blind spots on either side. The commanding officer of No. 500 Squadron, based at Detling, Kent, went one better than this. At the time of the Dunkirk evacuation his Anson also sported a 20 mm Hispano cannon–poking out of a hole specially cut in the rear fuselage floor on what had formerly been the site of the Elsan chemical lavatory. Apparently this 'secret weapon' achieved considerable success against unsuspecting German E-boats, and eventually several more of 500 Squadron's Ansons were similarly armed.

One particularly memorable incident in the annals of the Anson was an action which took place at low level over the Channel in June 1940. Three Ansons were attacked by nine Messerschmitt Bf 109s and not only did they success-

fully defend themselves, but also succeeded in shooting down two of the enemy and damaging a third. Two of the Anson crew members were wounded.

During that fateful summer there were other operational incidents scarcely less remarkable. In July 1940, for example, a Coastal Command Anson on reconnaissance shot down a Messerschmitt Bf 110 twin-engined fighter. Though 242 km/h (150 mph) or so slower than the Bf 110, the audacious 'Annie' intervened when its pilot discovered four of the German fighters machine-gunning British trawlers off the south coast. The ill-fated Bf 110 left the trawlers and came in for a beam attack, but the Anson's turret gunner kept his nerve and held his fire until he could be sure of a hit. In the same month another Anson displayed similar temerity by intervening in a melée and accounting for a Heinkel He 115 twin-engined seaplane and an He 111 bomber.

By the end of 1941, the Anson had been almost completely replaced in operational service with Coastal Command, but, thanks to its wonderful reliability, it was adopted at this time for another maritime duty–air/sea rescue–to undertake searches for ditched aircrew. It performed this valuable task for some two years until replaced by such types as the Vickers Warwick and Supermarine Spitfire.

Top: Anson Mk21 WJ561, a navigation trainer, was the last Anson to come off the production line. Above: an Anson of RAF Air Support Command in the 1960s. The Anson ended its days with the RAF as a communications aircraft

The Immortal Lanc

High-flying in paths of sunlight
O'er clouds the moon had kissed,
Black in the blood-red sunset,
Or grey in the morning mist –
Target or load or distance
Were all the same to you:
Through hell and flak you roared, and back
Above the stratocu.

The above lines, penned by an unknown poet, might well have been written as a salute to any of many types of World War II bombers, whether operating by night or day. But whatever aircraft might have originally inspired them, they do seem an eminently suitable tribute to one machine in particular: the Avro Lancaster, or, to give it the shortened name by which it was almost universally known in RAF circles, the 'Lanc'.

Marshal of the Royal Air Force Sir Arthur Harris, RAF Bomber Command's great wartime chief, once referred to the Lancaster as the 'greatest single factor in winning the war'. Be that as it may, it is an undeniable fact

[at least not during World War II]. It surpassed all other types of heavy bombers. It was easier to handle and there were fewer accidents with it. Throughout the war the casualty rate of Lancasters was always below that of other types.'

From 1942, when the Lancaster was put into operational service, until the end of the war in Europe, it hauled two-thirds of the total tonnage of bombs dropped by Bomber Command. It won battle honours during the early daylight raids on Augsburg, Le Creusot and Danzig, the attacks on the dams in western Germany and the sinking of the *Tirpitz*. By 1945, its efficiency and versatility made Bomber Command almost a 'Lancaster Command' and in April of that year, out of 1,609 aircraft with crews available daily, no fewer than 1,087 were Lancasters.

The Avro Manchester

The Lancaster story began in May 1936, when the Air Ministry, conscious of the growing threat of Nazi Germany, issued specification P.13/36 calling for a big twin-engined, second-generation monoplane bomber which

Right: 'S-Sugar' of 207 Squadron in flight. The first unit to receive the Manchester, 207 Squadron took it into action for the first time on 24/25 February 1941 when six aircraft attacked a cruiser at Brest. Below: The crew board a Manchester of the same squadron

that the mighty Lanc was the outstanding heavy night bomber to thunder its way across the pages of history in World War II.

Its main asset was its capability of carrying a greater bomb load than any contemporary night bomber – the equivalent of a whole Spitfire fighter or 15,000 lb of bombs; and even more when specially modified. To quote 'Bomber' Harris again: 'Its efficiency was almost incredible, both in performance and in the way it could be saddled with ever-increasing loads. It is astonishing that so small an aircraft as the Lancaster could take the 22,000 lb Grand Slam bomb, a weapon no other aircraft in the world could carry

would be an advance on even the best of the first-generation types—the Vickers Wellington, whose prototype had not then flown. Handley Page at first designed a twin Rolls-Royce Vulture-engined bomber based on P.13/36, but later abandoned this project in favour of four Rolls-Royce Merlin engines and produced the Halifax, which in its original production form was to specification 32/37. Avro, on the other hand, stuck to P.13/36 and built the twin Vulture-engined Manchester which first flew in July 1939.

Designed by Roy Chadwick and his team, the Manchester was ordered into production to specification 19/37 in July 1937—two years before the first prototype flew—and in November 1940 the new 'heavy' entered squadron service with Bomber Command's Lincolnshire-based No. 5 Group. From then on its career was continually dogged by numerous troubles, some involving production and supply, and others being inherent technical troubles. Worst headache was the complicated 24-cylinder X-type

in-line Vulture engine which, among other problems, developed insufficient power and was very prone to over-heating. Crashes—many of them fatal—due to engine failures and other technical defects were all too frequent and it became a standard quip among squadron personnel that Manchesters *had* to be based in Lincolnshire as it was the best forced-landing area available. Groundings of several days, even weeks, were not uncommon and it was due to such occurrences that No. 97 Manchester Squadron was nicknamed the '97th Foot' by a neighbouring Wellington squadron.

In June 1942, after a total of 1,269 individual sorties had been flown, the last Manchesters were withdrawn from operations, and no one was the least bit sorry to see them leave Bomber Command.

Meanwhile, by 1939, Roy Chadwick and his team had taken steps to insure against the possibility of the Vulture engine's failure by considering other power plants. Design projects evolved included the Manchester IC and IIA with two Bristol Centaurus radial engines, the Manchester III with four Merlins, and other variants with two Napier Sabre or two Bristol Hercules engines. The Manchester III project was first mooted in September 1939 and in mid-1940 Avro was authorised to go ahead with the construction of a prototype, the Merlin being already well-proven in such aircraft as the Hawker Hurricane and Supermarine Spitfire fighters and the Armstrong Whitworth Whitley bomber.

The adaptability of the existing Manchester's airframe facilitated speedy construction of the Mk III prototype, which embodied about three-quarters of the Mk I's components, including the triple-finned tail unit, and was

Below left: Ground crew attend to this 207 Squadron aircraft. The Manchester was plagued with mechanical problems throughout its service career and the squadron re-equipped with the more reliable Lancaster in March 1942.
Below: An early example of the Manchester, showing the original central tail-fin

specially serialled BT308. The main difference between the two variants lay in the III's modified wing of increased span and the two extra engines. This was modification enough to justify a change of name from Manchester to Lancaster.

Development and production

Powered by 1,145hp Merlin Xs, the Lancaster prototype first took to the air on 9 January 1941 at Ringway, near Manchester, piloted by Captain H. A. Brown, and later that month it went to the Aeroplane and Armament Experimental Establishment (A&AEE) at Boscombe Down, Wiltshire, for intensive flight trials. The engine/airframe combination proved to be a great success and it was decided to re-equip some of Bomber Command's existing twin-engined squadrons with it as soon as possible, starting with No. 5 Group. Accordingly, arrangements were made for the curtailment of Manchester production and a change over to the Lancaster at Avro and the second producer, Metropolitan Vickers, and construction of a second prototype was pressed forward with all possible speed.

Serialled DG595, the second prototype was a true Lancaster and differed considerably in detail design from BT308. Powered by 1,280hp Merlin XXs, it first flew on 13 May 1941 and was used during construction to try out production methods and fittings. During July and August 1941, while this machine was away at A&AEE for its preliminary RAF trials, Roy Chadwick focused his attention on a number of installation features which he knew could be improved. To speed progress, numbers of experimental department employees and design office draughtsmen were transferred to Avro's assembly plant at Woodford in Cheshire. The work was parcelled out and everyone had a definite job to do with Chadwick's personal instructions always before him: 'Make it simple, and try to imagine that six months hence you might have the job of repairing or overhauling this machine'. Drawing boards were sent down from the main drawing office at Chadderton, Manchester, and the draughtsmen actually worked on the benches alongside what were to be the first of the production Lancaster Is. Detail parts were made by hand on the spot and drawings issued immediately. Before the drawings were finished, the first five production machines were already taking shape on the assembly line and when the second prototype returned to Avro in September 1941 it was quickly modified to incorporate and test the improved installations.

The first production Lancaster I, L7527, made its maiden flight from Woodford on 31 October 1941, and by the end of the year several more had flown and the first squadron was already being equipped. The initial contracts were placed with Avro and 'Metrovick'. However, as demand grew and outstripped their production capabilities, the Lancaster Production Group was formed, eventually comprising the parent firm and four main 'daughter' firms in England: Metrovick at Manchester; Armstrong Whitworth Aircraft at Baginton near Coventry, (and from 1945 Bitteswell, Warwickshire); Vickers Armstrong at Castle Bromwich and Chester; and Austin Motors at Longbridge, Birmingham. To supplement its output at Manchester, Avro opened a vast shadow factory at Yeadon, near Leeds. The aforementioned firms were assisted in Lancaster production by more than 600 direct subcontractors. The group as a whole represented a labour force of some scores of thousands and a combined factory floor space of close on 20 million square feet. Peak production was reached by the group in August 1944

and in that one month 293 complete Lancasters were built, together with the appropriate quota of spare components, by a force of 131,745 workpeople.

Lancasters were also manufactured in Canada and would have been built in Australia too, had not plans been changed in fabour of the Lancaster's successor, the Lincoln. Altogether, 7,377 Lancasters were built, including prototypes, and all but 430 of them were produced in the UK. In addition spare parts representing an estimated 622 aircraft were built to maintain the Lancasters in service. The last Lancaster to be delivered, a Mk VII built by Austin Motors, was flight tested on 21 December 1945 at Elmdon, outside Birmingham.

Anatomy of the Lanc

A Lancaster consisted of about 55,000 separate parts, counting such composite items as engines and turrets as one and excluding nuts, bolts and rivets. About half a million manufacturing operations were involved, but, thanks to the Lancaster's comparatively simple structure,

Above: The second prototype Lancaster, pictured during flight trials. Right: A Lancaster I of 101 Squadron. The illustration of 'Uncle Joe' Stalin is derived from the aircraft's individual code letter J. Below: 50 Squadron converted to Lancasters from the Manchester in May 1942 and flew the type for the remaining years of the war

the total production time for each aircraft was kept to around 36,000 man-hours – well below that of either of its four-engined contemporaries, the Handley Page Halifax and the Short Stirling.

Spanning 31 m (102 ft) and beginning life at a normal gross weight of 27200 kg (60,000 lb), the Lancaster was an altogether pleasing looking aircraft and one which, when on the ground, always seemed sprightly and just raring to go. The fuselage was an all-metal structure of roughly oval cross-section, though distinctly narrower at the top than the bottom throughout most of its length. It was built in five separately-assembled main sections, its backbone being formed by pairs of extruded longerons located halfway down the cross-section of the three middle sections, cross beams between these longerons supporting the floor and forming the roof of the extremely capacious 10 m (33 ft) bomb bay. The wing was also built in five main sections, comprising a centre section of parallel chord and thickness, two tapering outer sections and two semi-circular wingtips. The wing structure comprised two spars, each consisting of a top and bottom extruded boom bolted to a single heavy-gauge web plate, the whole being covered by a flush-riveted aluminium alloy skin. The under-carriage comprised hydraulically-retractable mainwheels, each 1·67 m (5 ft 6 in) in diameter, and a fixed tailwheel – the saving in drag that would have resulted from a

Below: The Lancaster final assembly line at Woodford, Cheshire. In total, 6,949 Lancasters were built in the United Kingdom, plus a further 430 produced by Victory Aircraft in Canada

retractable tailwheel not being worth the weight and complication of the hydraulics. The engines were underslung, and the slim and altogether neat and compact appearance of the Merlin 'standard' power plants added greatly to the Lancaster's good looks and helped materially towards the all-round high performance, which included a top speed of 442 km/hr (275 mph) fully loaded at 4570 m (15,000 ft).

Fuselage layout of the Lancaster was orthodox with the nose gun turret above the comfortable prone position of the bomb aimer, who had an excellent view through an optically perfect circular window set into the Perspex chin blister. Above, behind, and to port was the pilot's position, high up in the raised canopy, with excellent vision all round. The back of the pilot's seat was armour-plated

Above: Lancasters silhouetted against the smoke and glowing target markers over Pforzheim, February 1945.
Below: Night take-off for a Lanc of 44 Squadron, Dunholme Lodge in January 1944

and beside it was a tip-up seat and behind that, on the starboard side, the flight engineer's panel and seat. Bullet-proof glass gave him a good view for fighting control, i.e. acting as lookout, telling the gunners where to fire and also telling the pilot when to take evasive action. Beside that, on the port side, was the navigator's seat and table, with plenty of space for the stowage of charts. Then came a bulkhead, and behind that, on the port side, the wireless operator's position just forward of the wing front spar,

with the astro-dome above. An armour-plated bulkhead afforded further protection and behind it a comfortable rest bunk was situated on the port side over the top of the crate for the oxygen bottles.

Behind the rear spar and near the entrance door, which was in the starboard side of the fuselage, were the dorsal and ventral turrets, and in the extreme tail the rear turret. All the turrets were of Frazer Nash design (except in special cases) and mounted a total of ten ·303 in Browning machine guns, the four in the tail being fed by ammunition tracks from boxes in the rear fuselage. The dorsal turret had two guides running in appositely named 'taboo tracks' to prevent the gunner from shooting off the Lancaster's fins, in the excitement of combat.

Operational debut

The distinction of being the first Lancaster squadron went to No. 44 Squadron at Waddington, whose veteran Handley Page Hampdens began to be replaced by the new heavy on Christmas Eve 1941. Some experienced 5 Group crews had been detached to Boscombe Down from mid-1941 onwards to gain experience on the Lancaster and to take part in the development flying programme, before

> During World War II the Lancaster flew a total of 156,192 operational sorties (116 of them under the temporary control of RAF Coastal Command). Of this total, 148,403 sorties were on bombing raids (108,264 at night), 2,929 were sea mining and most of the remainder were anti-submarine patrols. Lancaster losses were 3,349 missing and 487 destroyed or damaged.

helping to convert the squadrons. In mid-January 1942 No. 97 Squadron at Coningsby also started to re-equip. A month later this unit had 17 Lancasters, plus a single remaining Manchester, and with these it moved to Woodhall Spa. On 8 March No. 207 Squadron at Bottesford, Leicestershire, received its first Lancaster. The build-up was gathering momentum.

The Lancaster made its operational debut on the night of 3 March 1942 when four aircraft and crews of No. 44

Squadron, including Sqn Ldr J. D. Nettleton, one of the flight commanders, laid mines in the Heligoland Bight. A week later, on 10/11 March, Lancasters flew their first bombing mission when two from No. 44 Squadron, each carrying 5,050lb of small incendiaries, took part in a raid on Essen in the Ruhr.

Some structural weaknesses appeared in the Lancaster in its early days and in March 1942 a brand new Lancaster was sent to Boscombe Down for an intensive programme of diving trials. On 18 April, by which time the trials had reached an advanced stage, it failed to recover from one of its dives and plunged into the ground at Charlton, near Malmesbury, Wiltshire, killing its entire crew. Examination of the wreckage revealed that air loads had gradually been pulling rivets holding the upper wing surface skin, and on this particular flight a large panel of skin had finally lifted, causing loss of control. Precautionary checks made on other Lancasters brought to light other instances of pulled rivets, so a production modification was immediately put in hand.

Daylight raids

For the great majority of the people of Britain their first knowledge of the Lancaster came with the announcement of the daylight low-level precision attack on the MAN diesel engine works at Augsburg, in southern Germany, on 17 April 1942. Nos. 44 and 97 Squadrons were alerted for the mission, and in preparation for it they were ordered to make long-distance practice flights in formation to test the Lancaster's endurance. After heading south to Selsey Bill, they turned and flew to Lanark in Scotland, and then further north to Inverness where they feigned an attack just outside the town before returning to their Lincolnshire bases. Many complaints were received from members of the public accusing the RAF of low-level pranks. A poultry farmer in Scotland grumbled that as a result of the low flying his hens had stopped laying.

Twelve Lancasters, flying in two formations and practically at rooftop level, set out unescorted to make the attack on the MAN factory. Four of the leading formation were shot down by fighters, but the remainder carried on, despite formidable opposition from anti-aircraft fire, to attack their objective successfully with delayed-action bombs. Three more Lancasters were lost after they had

dropped their load, but the remaining five, all damaged, returned home safely, including the aircraft flown by Sqn Ldr J. D. Nettleton, whose part in the operation earned him the Victoria Cross.

News of this audacious raid came as a tonic to the British public after a period of major reverses – the sinking of HMS *Prince of Wales* and HMS *Repulse*, the Channel escape of the German warships *Scharnhorst* and *Gneisenau*, and the fall of Singapore.

From this time onwards, Lancasters became a household name and, apart from their regular job of bombing German industry by night (which included participation in the 'Thousand Bomber' raids on Cologne, Essen and Bremen in May/June 1942), they were used on many special operations, although, insofar as daylight raids

Left: The crew of a flak-damaged Lanc of 460 (RAAF) Squadron relax after a raid on Peenemunde on the night of 17/18 August 1943.
Below: This Lancaster fell victim to the elite JG2 'Richthofen'

Above left: A Lancaster II of 408 'Goose' Squadron takes off from its base at Linton-on-Ouse in 1943. Above right: An underside view of a 50 Squadron Lancaster in 1942

went, they were never again despatched on a task of comparable ambition and hazard.

Nevertheless, on 17 October 1942, another spectacular raid took place, partly in daylight, when 94 Lancasters from eight No. 5 Group squadrons had for their target the Schneider armament works at Le Creusot, France – or, in a few cases, the associated transformer and switching station at Montchanin. The raid involved up to ten hours' flying and only one aircraft was lost. Eighty-one Lancasters dropped their bombs at Le Creusot, but much of the

bombing overshot the Schneider works and the results were extremely disappointing. Enemy opposition was almost negligible and startled birds were the main danger, four Lancasters of No. 50 Squadron having their cockpit windows smashed as they roared at low level over France. One of the few bombers intercepted by the enemy was a Lancaster of No. 207 Squadron which lost formation due to engine trouble. This was attacked near the French coast by three German floatplanes, but good marksmanship by two of the Lancaster's gunners shot down two of the

for distance flown with the longest bomber operations of the war and it was remarkable that only two of the forty-odd Lancasters taking part were missing. A small force of Lancasters attacked the submarine yards at Flensburg at dusk on 28 July 1942 and this raid was more successful; an important shop in the yards was wrecked over an area of 40,000 square feet.

Hercules powerplants

By the early summer of 1943, the year which brought the beginning of real devastation to industrial Germany, the Lancaster I had been joined in service by two other versions. These were the Mk II, the only version to have radial engines (initially 1,735hp Bristol Hercules VIs, but

Left: 'Bombing up' a Lanc in September 1944. Maximum bomb load of the aircraft was 9980kg (22,000lb), which could be made up of mines, incendiaries, or bombs. Far left: Lancaster I coded VN-N of 50 Squadron which crashed at Thurlby while returning from a mine-laying mission on 19 September 1942

floatplanes and drove off the third. One of the five Lancasters which attacked the Montchanin objective released its bombs at only 150 feet and was damaged by the blast. Nevertheless it was flown safely home by its pilot, Flt Lt J. V. Hopgood, who thus survived to take part in and die in yet another famous Lancaster operation seven months later – the epic raid on the Möhne dam.

Exactly a week after the Le Creusot raid, Italy received its first daylight attack of the war when 5 Group sent 88 Lancasters to Milan, one of northern Italy's rich industrial towns and its most important railway centre. Seventy-four crews are known to have bombed the town and their efforts dotted it with fires and reduced the railway system to chaos. Italian fighters were active and one Lancaster was attacked five times by a Fiat CR 42 biplane. Its fifth attack slightly damaged the bomber's wing but the Lanc's gunners shot it down. Another Lancaster destroyed a Macchi 202. Three Lancs failed to return from the raid, one being claimed by the Italian defences and two by German fighters over northern France.

Still another notable attack delivered by day-flying Lancasters was made on 11 July 1942 against Danzig in Poland, although some of the bombers arrived after dark. The target, the submarine building yards, was not damaged, but neighbouring buildings were hit and considerable damage was caused to the town. Involving a round trip of 1,750 miles, this operation compared favourably

Hercules XVIs of similar power in the majority); and the Mk III, which was visually identical to the Mk I but had American Packard-built Merlin engines.

The Lancaster II was produced as an insurance against any interruption in the supply of Merlins. Two prototypes were ordered from Avro but only one (DT810) was completed and this first flew on 21 December 1941. Production of the Lancaster II was undertaken by Armstrong Whitworth and during its career the aircraft was sometimes fitted with a Frazer Nash FN64 ventral turret, like that carried by early Mk Is (and also some later Lancasters). Usually this turret mounted twin ·303in Browning guns, but sometimes a single ·5in Browning was installed instead. Bulged bomb doors, which allowed the inclusion of an 8,000lb blockbuster in the type's 14,000lb maximum bomb load, were a feature of the Lanc II and they became a standard fitment, also being introduced on some Mk Is and IIIs.

First unit to operate the Lancaster II was 61 Squadron at Syerston, Nottinghamshire, which, in the winter of 1942–43, received nine to supplement its Mk Is. Two initial sorties by Mk IIs, against Essen on the night of 11/12 January 1943, proved abortive as they could not reach the required operational ceiling, but five nights later the type went into action successfully against Berlin.

The crews of 61 Squadron's trials flight were not enamoured of their Lanc IIs, however, for although they

Avro Lancaster MK1 No.44 Squadron

Dimensions
Span 31 m (102 ft)
Length 21·1 m (69 ft 4 in)
Height 5·95 m (19 ft 7 in)

Performance
Maximum speed 460 km/h (287 mph)
Operational ceiling 6710 m (22,000 ft)
Operational range 2780 km (1,730 miles)

Engines
Four 1,280 hp Rolls-Royce Merlin XX, 22 or 24

Armament
Ten ·303 Browning machine-guns
Bomb load of up to 9980 kg (22,000 lb)

Loaded weight
Max take-off weight 30840 kg (68,000 lb)

Ten Lancaster captains and crew members were awarded the Victoria Cross in World War II. They were: Sqn Ldr I. W. Bazalgette of 635 Sqn, Wg Cdr G. L. Cheshire of 617 Sqn, Wg Cdr G. P. Gibson of 617 Sqn, Sgt N. C. Jackson of 106 Sqn, Plt Off N. C. Mynarski of 419 Sqn, Sqn Ldr J. D. Nettleton of 44 Sqn, Sqn Ldr R. A. M. Palmer of 109 Sqn, Flt Lt W. Reid of 61 Sqn, Capt E. Swales of 582 Sqn and Flt Sgt G. Thompson of 9 Sqn.

attained 24,000 ft lightly loaded on test, they struggled to reach 18,000 ft with a bomb load and were thus particularly vulnerable to the enemy's increasing night fighter and flak defences. Nevertheless, they were faster than the Merlin Lancs at lower altitudes, had a superior initial rate of climb and their air-cooled radial engines were reliable under fire, being less vulnerable to coolant leaks. On the other hand, their fuel consumption was greater than that of the Merlin Lancs and on long trips over the Alps to Italy left little or no margin. Due again to the ceiling limitations, there were some grim jests when the Lanc IIs were first given an Italian target – Turin, on 4/5 February 1943 – that their ceiling was below that of the Alpine peaks; happily the crews' fears were unfounded.

No. 61's Lancaster II flight was soon withdrawn, but in the spring of 1943 115 Squadron at East Wretham, Norfolk, in 3 Group and formerly flying Wellingtons, became the first homogeneous Lancaster II squadron. It received its first Lanc IIs in March and first used them operationally on the night of 20/21. Three squadrons of 6 (RCAF) Group – 426 'Thunderbird', 408 'Goose' and

Above: A Lancaster III in flight. Lancs were often engaged in daylight raids in the later stages of the war, particularly in support of the Normandy invasion

432 'Leaside' – based in Yorkshire began to operate Lanc IIs before the end of 1943 and in 3 Group the newly-formed 514 Squadron also received the Hercules-powered Lanc. Production of the type eventually reached 300, the last example coming off the production line at Armstrong Whitworth in March 1944.

'Paddle steamers'

Deliveries to the squadrons of the Packard Merlin-powered Lancaster III began at the end of 1942 and production continued, concurrently with that of the Mk I, until after the war. The number of Lanc IIIs delivered as such by the contractors – Avro (Manchester and Yeadon), Armstrong Whitworth and Metrovick – totalled 3,039 (for comparison the ex-works total of Lancaster Is was 3,425); but there were some conversions in service of Mk IIIs to Mk Is and vice versa. The transformation from one mark to another resulted merely from engine changes, usually on major overhaul, and some Lancasters flew with a mixture of British and American Merlins and in effect

became hybrid marks. Hamilton propellers with broad paddle-like blades, which originated from the Packard Merlins, were gradually fitted to most aircraft, giving improved take-off, climb and ceiling. They also led to the Lancs so equipped being nicknamed 'paddle steamers'.

The first Lancaster to fly with Packard Merlins was R5849, a Mk I, which, after delivery to Rolls-Royce in April 1942, was initially used for British Merlin XX development. American Merlin 28s were installed in this aircraft on 15 August 1942, for intensive development work, and this led to another Mk I (W4114) being similarly fitted in that same month for A&AEE trials at Boscombe Down. This second test-bed was redesignated as the official Lancaster III prototype. Production Lancaster IIIs used Packard-built Merlin 28s, with which coolant difficulties were experienced, and later Packard Merlin 38s or 224s, both of which were right up to Rolls-Royce standards. The engines were the only difference between the Mks I and III and performance-wise the two marks of Lanc were almost identical, although the American carburation system was superior and gave the aircraft a slightly more economical cruise performance. At this juncture it should be mentioned that the Lancaster I, having started life powered by Merlin XXs giving 1,280 hp for take-off, was given Merlin XXIIs of similar power and eventually 1,620 hp Merlin XXIVs as production progressed.

Lancaster IIIs began to reach the squadrons in December 1942 and thereafter those squadrons that had hitherto flown Mk Is operated Mk Is and IIIs side-by-side. Likewise the Heavy Conversion Units (HCUs) and Lancaster Finishing Schools (LFSs) flew both marks simultaneously; but as the Packard Merlin 28s tended to overheat quicker than the Rolls Merlins, the HCUs, whose

training syllabuses included successive take-offs and landings, preferred Mk Is.

The dams raid

Of all the Lancaster's exploits, none is more famous than the raid on the dams in western Germany made by Lancasters of 617 Squadron from Scampton, Lincolnshire, on the night of 16/17 May 1943. Their precise targets included the Möhne and Sorpe dams, both major dams on tributaries of the Ruhr river, and the Eder, another big dam further east. All three were, to varying degrees, important to the industrial and domestic life of the arms-producing Ruhr Valley, although not nearly as important as most historians have claimed in the past. Specially-modified Lancasters (Mk IIIs) were the only aircraft able to carry the ingenious 'bouncing bomb' designed by Sir Barnes Wallis of Vickers Armstrong specifically for this mission. No other aircraft on operations has carried a weapon like it. Actually a cylindrical mine resembling the cylinder at the front of a road-surface roller, the weapon, because of induced backspin, would skim across the surface of the water when released under predetermined conditions of speed and height, until coming into contact with the dam wall. It then rolled down the wall until it reached a depth sufficient to fire its hydrostatic pistols which in turn detonated its main explosive charge. By skimming the surface of the water when dropped, it foiled the enemy's elaborate anti-bomb and torpedo devices.

No. 617 Squadron was formed, specially for the dams raid, on 21 March 1943 under the command of Wg Cdr Guy Gibson, who had distinguished himself as an outstanding bomber and night fighter pilot during the early war years. Prior to taking over 617 Squadron he had, since 1942,

commanded No. 106 Squadron flying Manchesters and then Lancasters. He was granted the unprecedented privilege of selecting crews from other squadrons of Bomber Command and training in the completely new tactics which the mission demanded began five days after the squadron had formed, the entire project being shrouded in the utmost secrecy.

The crews, other than Gibson himself, were not told the targets until the briefing for the mission on 16 May. No. 617 put up 19 Lancasters for the raid and the crews were briefed to operate in three separate waves, the last of which acted as a mobile reserve from which individual aircraft could be directed to particular dams as necessary. The first Lanc took off from Scampton with its mine suspended from its cut-away belly shortly before 2130 hrs on 16 May and in due course the rest followed. 'After they had gone', wrote the squadron adjutant, 'Lincoln was silent once more; the evening mist began to settle on the aerodrome.' Wg Cdr Gibson's Lanc, the first to attack, released its mine over the Möhne lake at 28 minutes past midnight. Half an hour later, just after the fifth Lancaster had attacked, Gibson radioed back to England the pre-arranged code-word 'Nigger', indicating that the Möhne dam had been breached. (Nigger was the name of Gibson's black Labrador dog, beloved of all the squadron, who was killed by a car the day before the raid and buried at Scampton.)

The remaining aircraft of the Möhne formation then flew to the Eder dam. The first two mines failed to breach the dam, but shortly before 0200, when the third Lancaster had attacked, Gibson signalled the code-word 'Dinghy', indicating success with the second part of the operation. Other aircraft attacked the Sorpe and Schwelme dams but did not succeed in breaching them.

Left: The 22,000 lb 'Grand Slam' deep penetration bomb, the heaviest and most powerful of the war.
Top: A Grand Slam leaves a 617 Squadron Lancaster I (Special) over the Arnsberg viaduct on 19 March 1945.
Above: First victim of this mighty weapon was the Bielefeld railway viaduct, pictured after the raid on 14 March 1945

Left: Normal crew complement of the Lancaster was seven. Pictured above from top left are the bomb-aimer, pilot, flight engineer and navigator and below, from left, the wireless operator, mid-upper and rear gunners

Of the 19 Lancasters that took off for the dams raid with their 133 men, eight did not return. Five crashed or were shot down en route to their targets, two were destroyed while delivering their attacks, and another was shot down on the way home. Two more were so badly damaged that they had to abandon their missions. For his gallantry in this raid, Gibson–who afterwards wrote a vivid account of the whole operation in his book 'Enemy Coast Ahead'–received the Victoria Cross and 32 other members of the squadron were also decorated.

In one operation No. 617 Squadron–known from this time onwards as the 'Dam Busters'–had become famous and the decision was made to keep it in existence as a precision bombing unit. It was re-equipped with Lancasters of the standard type (Mk Is and IIIS, including some of the surviving dams raid Mk III [Special] Lancs) and returned to operations on 15/16 July 1943 with a raid on two power stations in northern Italy. All the aircraft landed at Blida in North Africa. On the return journey, on 24/25 July, Leghorn was attacked.

Path Finder Force

Meanwhile, on 15 August 1942, the Path Finder Force (PFF) was formed. Its role was guiding the main force of Bomber Command by identifying the target precisely and then illuminating it, so that 'marker' aircraft could drop incendiaries (or sky-marker flares above heavy cloud) as aiming points for the main force. Starting life with five squadrons–one from each operational group, including 83 Squadron with Lancasters from 5 Group–it itself achieved group status as No. 8 (PFF) Group in January 1943 and eventually became entirely equipped with Lancasters and Mosquitos, the most suitable aircraft for this demanding task.

By the spring of 1943 the main force had been largely re-equipped with Lancasters and Halifaxes, while the PFF already had Oboe-equipped Mosquitos and the first H2S-equipped heavies (Stirlings and Halifaxes) among its aircraft (Oboe and H2S being radar bombing aids). The command was now poised to deliver a whole series of pulverising blows on Germany, among which the failures would be much rarer than the successes–a complete reverse of the situation hitherto. The opening blow fell on Essen on the night of 5/6 March, when 140 Lancasters formed the last of three waves of the main force, which was led by a PFF force of eight Oboe Mosquitos and 22 Lancasters. This raid, which seriously damaged 300 acres of Essen, included 66 acres of industrial plant, heralded the so-called Battle of the Ruhr which lasted until the end of July. Duisburg, Dortmund, Bochum, Düsseldorf, Wuppertal, Oberhausen and Krefeld all appeared on the target list, as also did towns as widely separated from the Ruhr as Berlin, Stettin and Pilsen in the east, Munich, Stuttgart and Nuremburg in the south-east, Turin and Spezia in the south and Lorient and St Nazaire in the West. Lancasters visited them all.

The Battle of Hamburg

In late July and early August the great city of Hamburg came in for a series of body blows, including four major RAF night attacks and two supplementary attacks by USAAF bombers operating in daylight. Aided by H2S and also the new radar-jamming 'chaff', code-named *Window*, the RAF bombers raised a terrifying fire storm and wrought destruction so tremendous that it remained unsurpassed until the USAAF's B-29 fire raid on Tokyo on 9/10 March 1945.

The final onslaught of the Battle of Hamburg, on 2/3 August, was delivered in weather that was no less than appalling. Heavy thunderstorms occurred on 2 August and the crews, when briefed, were told that the weather was extremely bad and that cumulo-nimbus clouds covered the route up to 20,000ft. Above that height the sky was reported to be clear. Just how severe the weather conditions were can be gauged from a letter written by Fl Lt R. Burr, pilot of a No. 44 Squadron Lancaster. 'We took off one by one in a flurry of pounding rain, and found ourselves immediately in a huge cumulo-nimbus cloud. The airspeed indicator fluctuated by thirty miles per hour or more, and the rate of climb indicator wobbled crazily up and down. The aircraft was tossed and buffeted by the swirling currents of air and we could climb only very slowly as we edged painfully higher. Fifty hard-won feet would be lost in an instant as we hit a powerful down-draught and then just as suddenly we would gain fifty feet like a fast moving lift, as we were carried upwards by a stream of rising air.' With great difficulty Burr forced his Lanc to 16,000ft and then set course over the North Sea feeling glad that 'my wrists and arms were strong', for it was only by a tremendous effort that his aircraft could be kept on an even keel. At 17,000ft the Lanc was still in heavy cloud and would climb no higher. Presently lightning began to play around it and 'all the metal parts of the aircraft shone with the blue spikes of St Elmo's fire. . . . About a quarter of a mile to port was another aircraft flying on a parallel course. . . . It seemed to be a mass of flame and I realised that it, too, must be covered with St Elmo's fire. . . . I stared at this flying beacon and . . . suddenly, as I watched, a streak of lightning split the heavens. There was a huge flash and burning fragments broke away.' What remained of the aircraft plunged to earth.

Burr was among those who succeeded in dropping his bombs that night, but many did not. Some idea of the scale of devastation and slaughter at Hamburg can be gauged from the fact that the city suffered in four nights (i.e. the RAF's major attacks alone) what all Britain suffered from German air raids in the entire war. About 50,000 Germans were killed and nearly 40,000 injured. Upwards of 1,000,000 fled the striken city. More than half the houses or flats in Hamburg were destroyed and about half the factories were destroyed too.

Precision bombing techniques

On 17/18 August 1943, Bomber Command struck at the German V-weapons experimental centre at Peenemünde, on the shores of the Baltic and once again caused severe damage. A force of 597 four-engined bombers was despatched for the operation, which was directed by Gp Capt J. H. Searby, CO of No. 83 (PFF) Squadron, flying in Lancaster III 'W-William.' Despite the fact that enemy night fighters were much in evidence, he remained over the target throughout the attack, instructing the main force by means of radio telephone. The raid was doubly notable as being the first occasion when the master bomber technique (pioneered by Guy Gibson in the dams raid) had been applied to a major attack, and the first occasion upon which Bomber Command's famous 'red spot fire' marker bomb was operationally used.

For the RCAF 'Thunderbird' Squadron from Linton-on-Ouse, Yorkshire, the Peenemünde raid was its first operational mission with Lancaster IIs. The squadron put up nine aircraft and one skippered by the CO, Wg Cdr L. Crooks, failed to return. Five nights later, when Bomber Command struck at Leverkusen, 'Thunderbird' Lanc IIs had the honour of being the first RCAF aircraft to drop 8,000 lb blockbuster bombs.

On November 3/4 when Bomber Command sent 589 aircraft to Düsseldorf there were in the force 38 Lancaster IIs of 3 and 6 Groups, which had been equipped with the new blind-bombing radar aid known as G-H. Mosquitos fitted with G-H had already operated over Germany, but this was the first time that the device had been used by heavies in a major raid. The crews of the G-H Lancasters were detailed to attack the Mannesmann Steel Works which lay in the southern outskirts of Düsseldorf. Five aborted, two failed to return, 16 suffered G-H failure and joined the main force's area attack, while the remaining 15 attacked their special target according to plan. Although very little damage was done to the factory, the performance of G-H was seen to be most promising and the raid marked another important stage in the development of precision bombing techniques. No. 3 Group became G-H specialists later in the war and among their main achievements with the blind-bombing aid was a sustained all-weather attack, in July and August 1944, on Hitler's flying bomb sites in Northern France.

Target Berlin

The winter of 1943–44 saw the heavies embroiled in the Battle of Berlin and into this campaign, on 26/27 November, went the RCAF's 'Leasides', making their first Lancaster II sorties. It was the third raid of the current series on the 'Big City' and in the two months or so that followed, the 'Leasides' hit Berlin nine more times. Judging by the experiences of two 'Leaside' crews during that period, it seems that the enemy, in an attempt to save his capital and homeland, was experimenting with something radically new in the way of night-fighter tactics. On the way out over Holland on 2/3 January, Lancaster 'E-Easy' (pilot Plt Off Tom Spink) was attacked head-on and considerably damaged by, of all things, a four-engined Focke-Wulf Kurier; while in a later raid 'B-Baker' got back to base at East Moor, Yorkshire, after having been similarly jumped and badly mauled by a Focke-Wulf Condor, the Kurier's peacetime antecedent. Spink and his navigator both put up a particularly good show in the above-mentioned Berlin mission and were each rewarded with the DFC. Another 'Leaside' pilot who earned a DFC with a cool-headed bit of flying on the same operation was Plt Off J. McIntosh. The following are excerpts from this pilot's report of what transpired aboard 'U-Uncle' shortly after dropping the bomb load: 'Just after we turned for home . . . the rear gunner (Sgt L. R. Bandle) spotted a Bf110. The enemy and my two gunners opened fire at the same instant. Cannon shells hit our aircraft like sledge hammers. The gunners scored hits on the 110's port engine and cockpit and the fighter went down, burning fiercely. All this happened within five seconds. Meanwhile my control column had been slammed forward (the elevator had been hit), putting the aircraft into a near-vertical dive . . . by putting both feet on the instrument panel, one arm around the control column, and the other hand on the elevator trim, then hauling back with every ounce of strength while trimming fully nose up, I managed to pull out of the dive at about 10,000 ft (13,000 ft below bombing height). My compasses were unserviceable, the rudder controls had jammed, and I could get very little response from the elevators. I still had to wrap both arms around the control column to maintain height. . . .

'We were now far behind the rest of the bombers, and our only hope was to stay in the cloud-tops and take our chances with the severe icing we were encountering. Fighter flares kept dropping all around us and the flak positions *en route* were bursting their stuff at our height, but the fighters couldn't see us in that cloud. . . . My navigator took astro fixes and kept us away as much as possible from defended areas. . . . We had been losing a lot of fuel from the starboard inner tank, but enough remained to take us to Woodbridge (a big emergency landing ground in Suffolk . . .).

'About seventy miles out to sea I let down through cloud, experiencing severe icing, then levelled off when I broke through. . . . The aircraft was now becoming very sluggish, and only with difficulty was I able to hold height. I detailed the crew to throw out all our unnecessary equipment and to chop out everything they could. This considerably lightened the aircraft and made it easier to control. I then ordered the crew to stand by for ditching, just in case. . . . The navigator headed me straight for Woodbridge, on Gee. . . .

'I used all the runway and felt the kite touch down on our port wheel. . . . It rolled along until the speed dropped to about 30 mph, then I settled down more on the side of the starboard wheel, did half a ground-loop, and stopped . . . I shut down the engines, got out, and took a look.

'Both starboard engine nacelles were gone; the hydraulics were smashed and twisted; two large tears were in

The last Lancaster in Coastal Command at a farewell ceremony at RAF St Mawgan, Cornwall, on 15 October 1956, before flying to Wroughton to be scrapped

the starboard wing near the dinghy stowage; the dinghy was hanging out; the starboard fuel jettison sac was hanging out; the tailplane was riddled with cannon and machine gun fire; the fuselage had five cannon holes through it (three of the shells had burst inside, near the navigator); there were two cannon holes in the rear turret (one of these shells had whistled almost the entire length of the fuselage before exploding); there were hundreds of holes of all sizes in the kite; every prop blade had at least one hole in it, one being split down the middle; the starboard outer oil tank was riddled, and the starboard tyre was blown clean off. . . . But nobody was injured. It had been a good trip until we were attacked by the fighter.'

And the fighter? Both of 'Uncle's' gunners, Sgts L. R. Bandle and A. F. Dedaux, had opened fire simultanously at 100 yards range, and loosed 500 rounds at it without taking their thumbs off the firing buttons. The enemy's port engine caught fire just as he broke away. He went into a succession of dives and half-hearted pull-outs, finally spinning out of control until lost to view.

More powerful Merlins

A little-known variant of the mighty Lanc which saw limited service in 1944 was the Mk VI, which had the more powerful Merlin 85/87 series engines, each developing 1,635 hp. Only a handful of Mk VIs were produced, all of them being converted by Rolls-Royce from standard Mk IIIs. The first two (DV170 and DV199) were converted in June and July 1943, but the next one (JB675), converted in November that year, was officially regarded as the prototype. This machine, and some later examples, were used for Service trials at Boscombe Down and the Royal Aircraft Establishment at Farnborough, Hampshire and in 1944 a few Mk VIs were allotted to the Path Finder Force for operational trials. Nos. 7 and 635 Squadrons at Oakington, Cambridgeshire and Downham Market, Norfolk respectively, did most of the flying, the Lanc VIs performing useful work on diversionary and master bomber duties, for which purpose they carried the latest H2S radar, numerous radio and radar-jamming devices, and target indicators. Nose and dorsal turrets were removed and the Merlin 85/87 series engines in their annular cowlings resembled slim radial engines; four-bladed paddle-type propellers were fitted.

Reports by crews varied, but one pilot, Flt Lt G. A. (Tony) Roome, DFC, of No. 635 Squadron, had this to say about the Lanc VI: 'The engines were very much more powerful, giving about 1,750hp each for take-off, but there was always the sneaking suspicion that they weren't very reliable. This was accentuated by the way they ran very rough and the fact that they used to surge and hunt, making synchronisation impossible. Also the ground crew fitters used to call them all the names under the sun. Thus, in spite of the better performance, the Lanc VI was not as sought-after as might be imagined.'

The Mk VI was withdrawn from operations after November 1944, but the experience greatly reduced teething troubles during the development of the stretched Lancaster Mk IV, which was later renamed the Lincoln.

Canadian Lancasters

The only other mark of Lancaster to see active service during World War II was the Canadian-built Mk X, which was selected early in 1942 for production by Victory Aircraft, a company formed by the National Steel Corporation of Canada. This version was fitted with Packard-built Merlin 38 or 224 engines, and the 'first off'

(KB700 – aptly named 'The Ruhr Express') was ferried to Britain in September 1943 by a crew from No. 405 'Vancouver' Squadron, RCAF, a Path Finder Force unit. It flew its first operational sortie on 22/23 November, when it was detailed to attack Berlin. Engine trouble caused the Lanc to return early, but five nights later it set out again for Berlin and this time made the trip in fine style. Eventually twelve RCAF bomber squadrons flew Lanc Xs on operations in Europe; total production was

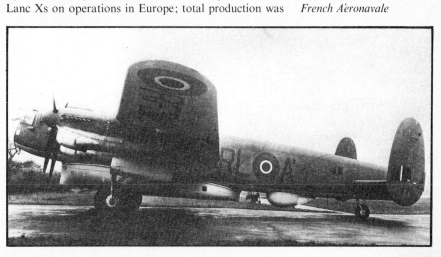

430 and by the end of the war they were leaving the Victory plant at a rate of one per day.

By 1944 Lancasters had largely replaced the Halifaxes and Stirlings as the backbone of Bomber Command. Their epic operations in 1944–45 alone were legion. They bludgeoned Berlin a dozen times, scored one of the air

Below: The ASR III air-sea rescue version of the Lancaster, showing the underslung airborne lifeboat.
Bottom: The first of several Lancasters supplied post-war to the French Aéronavale

Avro Shackleton MK 3 Phase 2
No. 206 Squadron

Dimensions
Span 36·5 m (119 ft 10 in)
Length 26·6 m (87 ft 4 in)
Height 7·1 m (23 ft 4 in)

Engines
Four 1,960 hp Rolls-Royce Griffon 57A

Performance
Maximum speed 420 km/hr (260 mph)
at 3650 m (12,000 ft)
Maximum range 5890 m (3,662 miles)
at 320 km/hr (200 mph)

Weights
Basic weight 26760 kg (59,000 lb)
Loaded weight 43320 kg (95,500 lb)

war's classic strokes of deceit with their invasion fleet spoof in the Channel on D-Day, flooded the Wehrmacht units on Walcheren island by breaching a dyke at West-kapelle, blocked the Saumur railway tunnel and destroyed the German battleship *Tirpitz* in Tromsö fjord, Norway–the two last-named operations utilising Sir Barnes Wallis's 12,000 lb Tallboy earthquake bomb. Their greatest weight-lifting feat of all was first demonstrated on 4 March 1945, when a No. 617 Squadron Lancaster I (Special), flown by Wg Cdr C. C. 'Jock' Calder, dropped on the Bielefeld Viaduct a bomb whose weight compared favourably with the basic weight of the carrier aircraft–the ten-ton Grand Slam, yet another brainchild of Sir Barnes Wallis. No other aircraft dropped as heavy a bomb or bomb load in World War II, not even the American Boeing B-29.

If the lifting ability of the Lancaster was remarkable, its flying characteristics were only slightly less so. Aero-dynamically superb in every way, it possessed the light handling qualities of much smaller aircraft. With a bomb load it was scarcely heavier on the controls than when empty. Yet its structure was unusually robust, enabling it to withstand the severe aerodynamic stress of a dive, loop, or roll, besides extensive battle damage. One No 44 Squadron Lanc, flying through flak, was blown on to its back by a near miss and eventually pulled out of the dive almost at ground level. Dozens of under-wing rivets had torn out; and the dihedral, visibly uneven in the early light next morning, would have suited an elastic powered, balsa and tissue flying model.

Combats with jets

A drama enacted thousands of times over war-torn Europe was the heavily-laden yet still nimble Lanc being 'stood on its ear' while corkscrewing violently to evade a night-fighter. In daylight, tactics were very different. On 31 March 1945, when the Luftwaffe made its first and last large-scale interception by day of a Canadian heavy bomber force. Lacking fighter cover because of a timing error, 6 Group's Lancaster gaggle was singled out over Hamburg for a concentrated attack by about 30 Messer-schmitt Me 262s–Germany's first operational jet inter-ceptors–each piloted by a holder of the Knight's Cross of the Iron Cross. The Lancasters fought back as never before. Probably for the first time in combat their Brown-ing ·303s blazed away from *all three* turrets at once. In all there were 78 encounters and 28 crews reported one or more combats with the pack of jets. Five Lancasters fell, but at least four and possibly seven Me 262s also went down in the biggest air-to-air battle fought by a Bomber Com-mand formation in daylight.

Perusal of dusty squadron records brings to light many long-forgotten tales of Lancaster exploits, but few can claim to be more hair-raising than this 'story of suspense' from the archives of No. 300 (Polish) Squadron, a unit of No. 1 Group, based at Faldingworth in Lincolnshire. Lancaster III 'J-Jig', piloted by Flt Sgt Z. Stepian, was one of more than a thousand aircraft bombing a target at Emieville, near Caen, on 18 July 1944, when flak badly damaged it. The rear gunner, Flt Sgt M. Zentar, was rotat-ing his turret searching for fighters at the time and the blast swung the turret beyond its usual position, ripped open the door and sucked him out of his seat. He fell out, but his left foot jammed in the doorway, and there he hung head downwards. The dorsal gunner and the flight engineer went to his aid but could not pull him in. His foot began to slip out of the shoe, so one of them grabbed his trousers, which, however, began to tear. The flight engineer then did a risky piece of work; he clambered out (the aircraft was now over the sea), precariously held in place and looped a length of rope round the rear gunner which he then made fast to the seat. He then returned to his task of nursing the damaged Lancaster back to base. The Lanc limped home with the rear gunner hanging head down from the tail, and those watching on the airfield saw him swing his head to one side to avoid hitting the ground as the bomber touched down. He was bleeding from ears and mouth, but was not badly hurt. He was subsequently able to boast of being the only man to have flown upside-down from Caen to Great Britain. Sgt J. Pialucha, the flight engineer, was given the immediate award of the Conspicuous Gallantry Medal for his outstanding courage and initiative.

By the end of the war in Europe there were 58 squadrons wholly equipped with Lancasters, including all 14 squad-

Below: A Shackleton Mk 1A of 269 Squadron, which equipped with Shackletons in early 1952 and flew the type after being renumbered 210 Squadron until 1971

Bottom: A Lancaster Mk VII, basically a Mk I with earlier Mk I/III modifications and a Martin dorsal turret. None of the 180 Austin-built Mk VIIs saw war service; this gunless example is pictured in the markings of 20 Maintenance Unit

The Lancaster's direct descendant and successor in RAF service was the Avro Lincoln, which served from 1945 until 1955. Powered by four Rolls-Royce Merlin 85s, it reached a maximum speed of 319mph at 18,500ft and had a range of 1,470 miles. A Lincoln derivative and the last of Lancaster line, the Avro Shackleton was developed as a specialised maritime patrol aircraft for RAF Coastal Command, replacing the Lancaster in this role. It served with fifteen squadrons and was produced in three marks. The South African Air Force also received the Shackleton in 1957. The latest version of the Shackleton, the AEW Mk 2, serves with 8 Squadron, RAF.

A Shackleton Mk 2, last derivative of the Lancaster to see RAF service. A modified version of the Mk 2 with a large ventral radome under the forward fuselage still operates as an airborne early warning aircraft with the designation AEW Mk 2

rons of No. 1 Group, the 11 squadrons of 3 Group, 17 squadrons of 5 Group, eight squadrons of 6 (RCAF) Group, and eight squadrons of 8 (PFF) Group (including two detached from 5 Group). Last operational missions in which Lancasters took part were on 25 April 1945, when Hitler's mountain retreat, the 'Eagle's Nest', and the associated SS barracks at Berchesgaden were bombed; and the following night when U-boat fuel-storage tanks at Vallo (Tönsberg) in Oslo fjord were bombed and part of Oslo fjord itself (off Horten) mined. The Lancs then turned to repatriating British ex-prisoners of war (Operation Exodus) and dropping food to the starving Dutch (Operation Manna). It was on this happy note that the war for the mighty Lancaster ended.

Peacetime tasks

VE-Day found plans already made for Lancasters to operate in the Far East against Japan as Tiger Force. Two Lancasters were fitted experimentally with large saddle tanks on the fuselage for long-range evaluation and flight refuelling experiments were performed with others. The atom bomb put an end to the plans for Tiger Force, but after the war the Lancaster continued to give good service

with the RAF, and under a new tropicalised standard many examples bore the suffix FE, signifying Far East. Several Lancasters were employed as engine test-beds and on other experimental work, some being civilianised.

Many Lancaster Mk IIIs were converted for use by Coastal Command, first as ASR IIIs and later as GR IIIs, for air-sea rescue and general reconnaissance respectively. Bomber Command continued to use Lancasters until sufficient Lincolns became available to replace them, its last first-line Lanc squadron being No. 49 which relinquished the last of its Lancs early in 1950. However, the last Bomber Command Lancaster to be retired was one of a small number of Mk Is specially converted after the war for photo-reconnaissance and employed by No. 82 Squadron chiefly in Africa (PA427, a PR1, withdrawn in December 1953). Coastal Command's last first-line Lancasters (they were also the last in first-line service with the RAF) were MR (formerly GR) 3s of Nos. 37 and 38 Squadrons based in Malta. The last Lancaster MR (RF273) was flown back to England and retired in February 1954. However the Lancaster MR3 continued in service with the School of Maritime Reconnaissance at St Mawgan, Cornwall, until October 1956 when the last example (RF325) was withdrawn - it was the RAF's last Lanc to be retired from a normal working career.

Canadian-built Lancaster Xs flew back to Canada in mid-1945, were 'mothballed' by the RCAF and were brought out of storage as required for a variety of roles, including maritime reconnaissance and photo-survey. The last RCAF Lancasters to be withdrawn from use were three aircraft of No. 408 Squadron, in April 1964.

Today several Lancasters are preserved as museum pieces in various parts of the world, and in Britain two examples are airworthy, including the well-known PA474, built in 1945 as a basic Mk I bomber, but later modified for photo-reconnaissance duties. Adopted by the Ministry of Defence in 1963, it was restored to represent a wartime Lancaster and has long sported the markings KM-B of Sqn Ldr Nettleton's Lancaster of Augsburg raid fame.

Fighting Canuck

The CF-100 was the first major warplane to be designed and built in Canada

Avro Canada CF-100s of the Royal Canadian Air Force in formation, showing the type's pre-1958 natural metal finish

Often unofficially called the Canuck, the CF-100 was the first major combat aircraft ever designed and produced entirely by Canada. It put that nation in the very forefront of modern fighter development, but its successor, the CF-105 Arrow, was cancelled just as it was getting into production so the CF-100 remains Canada's only home-grown combat aircraft of real significance.

After World War II it was clear that there was no existing fighter suited to the task of defending Canada. The country is larger than the United States and airfields good enough to serve as military bases were in 1945 often more than 1000 km (620 miles) apart. Though the United States was eventually to produce the F-89 Scorpion for similar duties, the Canadian Air Staff wrote their own specification and issued it in October 1946. It called for an interceptor more capable than any previously seen. It had to be jet propelled, and have all-round flight performance adequate for the coming transonic era. It had to have a crew of pilot and radar navigator, and sufficient fuel for missions longer in distance than any previous fighter could fly. It had to carry radar for night and all-weather interceptions, with powerful modern armament. It also had to be able to use short runways, climb rapidly and have excellent manoeuvrability at low airspeeds. It was an extremely challenging requirement, and around it grew a complete

industry, with capability in both airframes and engines. The airframe company had been named Victory Aircraft at Toronto, and in 1945 was producing the Avro Lancaster bomber and York transport. It was renamed Avro Canada in 1945, and soon showed its immense technical skill by producing the first aircraft ever designed as a short-haul jetliner, the C.102 Jetliner, flown a month after the first Comet in August 1949. In parallel it produced the Avro CF-100 for the Royal Canadian Air Force.

Rapid development

The first prototype was rolled out amid deep snow and flown for the first time on 19 January 1950. Compared with previous fighters it was extremely large and impressive. It had a glossy black finish and bore the letters FB-D and fin serial number 18101. To get it into the air before its new Canadian engines were ready it was powered by two of the first British axial turbojets, special sub-types of the Rolls-Royce Avon RA.3 rated at 2948 kg (6,500 lb) static thrust each. The engines were mounted on each side of the long, slim fuselage, forming an extremely broad central portion which generated one-third of the total lift. It put the engines directly above the low-mounted unswept wing, which carried powerful double-slotted flaps, airbrakes and powered ailerons. Pilot and navigator

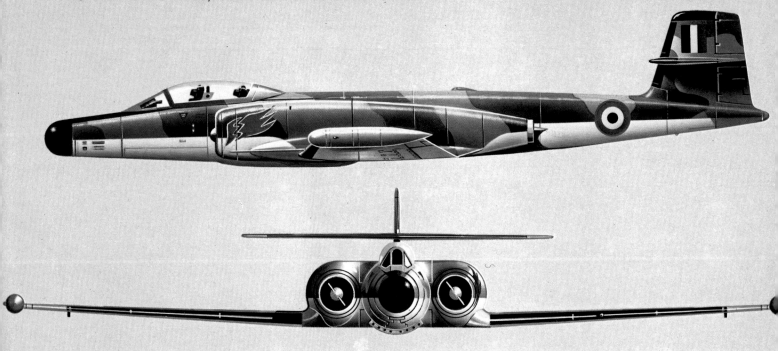

Bearing its former RCAF markings and camouflage, this privately-owned CF-100 is pictured at its base in Duxford, Cambridgeshire

sat in tandem ejector seats, the tailplane was mounted high on the squarish fin, with full powered controls, and the steerable nose gear and tall main landing gear all had twin wheels to carry the CF-100's considerable weight. Inside the fuselage was ample room for a vast quantity of fuel, for a range exceeding 4000 km (2,500 miles), and for the retracted mainwheels inboard of the engines.

Development was very satisfactory, and the new engine company, Orenda Engines Ltd—also located at Malton, Toronto, and likewise a member of the British Hawker Siddeley Group—made good progress with their Orenda axial turbojet which ran in 1949 and before the end of that year had passed most of its Type Test schedules. On 20 June 1950, as the black prototype continued tests with streamlined pods (fuel tanks or rocket launchers) on its wing-tips, Avro Canada flew the first all-Canadian aircraft in history, the first of ten service-test CF-100 Mk 2 aircraft powered by two 2720 kg (6,000 lb) thrust Orenda 2 engines. One of this batch was a Mk 2T conversion trainer with dual controls.

In September 1950 the RCAF had placed a contract for 124 CF-100 Mk 3 fighters, and these quickly filled the Malton plant. Essentially similar to the Mk 2, they differed mainly in having full combat equipment. This was not regarded as the definitive equipment because the RCAF was in touch with the USAF and the US company Hughes Aircraft, which had suddenly leaped into prominence as leaders in all-weather interception systems. Hughes, which supplied the E-1 fire-control system for the CF-100 Mk 3, knew that it was only a stop-gap, though it was as good as anything in the USAF at that time. The radar was the APG-33, and its small scanner allowed the Mk 3 to have a pointed nose. In the underside of the forward fuselage was a pack containing the formidable armament of eight 12·7 mm (0·5 in) guns, linked with a fire control system which included the radar and an autopilot. The Mk 3 was pleasant to fly, very popular and at a normal (clean) gross weight of 15420 kg (34,000 lb) could reach 1030 km/h (640 mph) and climb at over 3000 m (10,000 ft) per minute. But this mark was cut back to 70 aircraft to hasten the switch in production to the definitive Mk 4 version.

Outstanding interceptor

The CF-100 Mk 4 was a truly outstanding aircraft, and probably the best all-weather interceptor in the world in 1953. Much of its forward fuselage was redesigned to accommodate the extremely large and complex Hughes E-4 fire control system, produced for the two-seat

Avro Canada CF-100 of the Belgian Air Force

Dimensions
Span 17·7 m (58 ft)
Length 16·7 m (54 ft 2 in)
Height 4·76 m (15 ft 6½ in)

Engines
Two Orenda Mk II turbojets, each of
3175 kg (7,000 lb) thrust

Performance
Maximum speed 1110 km/h (690 mph)
Operational ceiling 16461 m (54,000 ft)
Range 4000 km (2,500 miles)

Armament
Eight 0·5 in machine guns or 77 2·75 in
rockets in ventral and wingtip pods

Canadian interceptor as the MG-2 with special provision for rocket armament. Hughes and the USAF had devised a method of automatic 'collision course' interception firing a salvo of 70 mm (2·75 in) FFARs (folding-fin aircraft rockets), the latter being popularly known as 'mighty mice'. In the Mk 4 the guns were supplemented by 58 FFARs carried in pods on the wing tips, which were jettisonable after the rockets had been fired. If required the gun pack could be removed and replaced by a pack containing a further 48 FFARs. The Mk 4A had 2948 kg (6,500 lb) Orenda 9 engines with alcohol anti-icing sprays on a windmill like a small propeller on the nose bullet. The whole airframe had thermal de-icing along all leading edges.

Despite its great bulk, and the fact the fattest part was in line with the unswept wing (the very opposite of the shape dictated by the 'Area Rule' for minimum transonic drag), the CF-100 often demonstrated its ability to exceed the speed of sound in a dive. When the Mk 3 joined 445 Sqn at North Bay in 1953 the Canadian fighter was the fastest aircraft in service in the British Commonwealth apart from the swept-wing Sabre. When the 3400 kg (7,500 lb) Orenda 11 was introduced in the CF-100 Mk 4B, the big Canadian fighter could outrun even a Sabre, despite having unswept wings and tail, and its take-off and climb were markedly superior. The Mk 4B usually had the rocket pack instead of guns, and all B models, and many 4As, had an extremely large single-piece canopy in place of the normal two-section assembly. Like the F-89D Scorpion, the Mk 4 family had a bluff nose with a large radome (which stood up well to intensive operation at jet speeds through some of the worst weather in the world), and its all-round performance as an all-weather interceptor was outstanding. No fewer than 510 of various Mk 4 models were delivered and they equipped at peak 21 squadrons of the RCAF in Canada and Western Europe.

An in-flight view of a CF-100, showing the wide cross-sectional area which belied its ability to exceed the speed of sound in a dive

In 1952 the CF-103 had been planned with swept wings and tail, but this was abandoned in 1954 and had never been regarded as anything but a stop-gap pending the definitive Mach 2 interceptor, which by 1955 was taking shape as the even larger and much more powerful CF-105 Arrow. The Arrow was planned with guided-missile armament, and Avro Canada worked with Hughes to adapt the CF-100 to the AIM-4C and -4D Falcon missiles (then designated GAR-98 or GAR-1). A different team worked with Douglas and Raytheon, and with other Canadian companies, to mate the CF-100 with the Sparrow II, a larger and longer-ranged air-to-air missile. As a temporary measure, Avro produced a long-span CF-100 with extended wing tips, giving improved take-off and altitude performance at the increased weights over 18144 kg (40,000 lb) of the later Mk 4 versions on the longest missions. This model, called CF-100 Mk 5, had parallel-chord extra sections on the tips which increased span from 15·85 to 17·68 m (52 ft to 58 ft). On the tips were larger rocket pods each housing 52 FFARs. There were various small changes, and while production of new Mk 5s continued to bring the total for all models up to 692, about 180 Mk 4s were also rebuilt to Mk 5 standard.

Canucks to Belgium
The last 53 aircraft off the Malton line were for the Royal Belgian Air Force, forming that country's first all-weather interceptor force. Like all front-line RCAF CF-100s from about 1958 the Belgian aircraft were painted in typical two-colour camouflage, the original deliveries all having been unpainted. The last aircraft was delivered in early 1958, and though the CF-105 flight programme was then under way, it was clear there would be a gap between the two programmes as far as the workforce was concerned. This gap was to some degree eased by the need to rebuild and update large numbers of CF-100s until the early 1960s, and in particular by the urgent need to strengthen the wings of the long-span Mk 5 which had suffered structural failure in high-g manoeuvres. This was a temporary problem but it marred an otherwise exemplary safety record in combat duty.

In view of the gigantic CF-105 programme, Avro Canada did not push especially hard for further models of CF-100, but development plans had been completed for the Mk 6 with afterburning Orenda engines and Sparrow II missiles. Orenda did much running with the afterburning Orenda 11R, rated at 4080 kg (9,000 lb), and this flew in a neat installation in a CF-100. For training purposes a number of CF-100s were converted to 5M standard with modified radar to serve in the target-illuminating mode for Sparrow II missiles (the Sparrow II was one of the chief missiles for the CF-105).

Canadian Air Defence
When on 20 February 1959 Prime Minister Diefenbaker cancelled the entire CF-105 Arrow programme he dealt a death blow to Avro Aircraft, as Avro Canada had become, and to the defence capability of Canada. Never again was Canada to be self-sufficient in combat aircraft, and the only fighters used since by the Canadian Armed Forces have been second-hand CF-101 Voodoos, licence-built F-104 Starfighters and F-5 Freedom Fighters, all of which have very limited capability and make no pretence to defending Canadian airspace. Today Canada is again looking at the need to defend against aircraft attack – a subject thought outmoded when the CF-105 was cancelled – but has no option but to buy or build a foreign aircraft. As for the great CF-100, this gradually became obsolescent despite the fact that in many respects other than top speed it was superior to the CF-101B Voodoo bought second-hand from the USAF. Inability to update the old Mk 4 and 5 aircraft with guided missiles, through absence of action at the right time, led to the retirement of nearly all the Canadian interceptor force by 1965, and withdrawal of the Canadian all-weather forces from Western Europe. Over 100 CF-100s served in various trials programmes, and as ECM (electronic countermeasures) platforms carrying chaff pods, jammers and other equipment intended to prepare the way for attack by such small tactical machines as the CF-104 and CF-5. One CF-100 has been retained by Pratt & Whitney Aircraft of Canada for use as the flying testbed of the JT15D civil turbofan, mounted in a pod under the fuselage. The CF-100 is exceptionally well suited to such work, having large ground clearance, long endurance and the capability of carrying an observer and extensive instrumentation.

The Legless Air Ace

The airman who overcame severe disabilities to become one of RAF's leading fighter pilots

Few men become legends in their own lifetime: fewer still overcome a severe physical handicap by sheer force of character and prove to themselves and to the world that life does not end with tragedy. One such man is Group Captain Sir Douglas Bader.

Born in St John's Wood, North London, on 21 February 1910, Douglas Robert Steuart Bader proved an energetic child, who excelled at sport and had a powerful sense of adventure. His father, a major in the Royal Engineers during World War I, was wounded by shrapnel in 1917 and, although seemingly recovered, he died of his wound in 1922. His mother's sister, meanwhile, had married a Royal Air Force pilot, Cyril Burge, who had flown with the RFC and RAF during the war, and the stories he told his young nephew fired an already active imagination. It was not surprising therefore, that after his formal education at St Edward's School, Oxford, he decided to join the Royal Air Force.

With help and advice from his uncle, now a Squadron Leader, who was also the personal assistant to Air Chief Marshal Sir Hugh Trenchard, Chief of the Air Staff, Bader managed to gain a prize cadetship to RAF Cranwell. It was September 1928 and he was eighteen years old.

Bader was taught to fly in the Avro 504, was assessed an 'above average' pilot and in his spare time represented Cranwell at cricket, rugby, hockey and boxing. Almost two years after his entry, on 26 July 1930, he was commissioned and, as a fully trained pilot, was posted to 23 Squadron at RAF Kenley. The squadron was equipped with Gloster Gamecock single-seat fighters. The world was now at his feet. He was well liked by his companions, a good pilot, a superb sportsman and his wish to fly and be a fighter pilot had been fulfilled.

Bulldog crash

He represented the RAF in various sports and was even chosen to fly in the Hendon air pageant in the combined aerobatics event just before his squadron began to convert to Bristol Bulldog fighters. Then came tragedy. On 14 December 1931 he was asked to give a demonstration aerobatic flight by some pilots at a private flying club. When he declined, someone made a comment which Bader could not ignore. He took his Bulldog into the crisp wintery sky, then dived down to show the rude club member what flying was all about. But he made a slight misjudgement. The Bulldog's left wing-tip touched the ground and the little biplane crashed, seriously injuring Douglas Bader.

The crash robbed him of both legs and, it seemed, of a most promising flying career. After months in hospital, being several times on the brink of death, he eventually rallied and became determined to face life again. Fitted with two artificial metal legs, Bader soon began to walk again, but sadly the RAF had no place for him and so he had to face a completely new life in 'civvy street'. These were the most difficult years but he survived the hardships, married and by 1939 was working for the Shell Oil company. When war came again to Europe, Bader immediately offered his services to the RAF. In spite of his handicap, he so impressed those he saw during his various interviews

Below: the aerobatic team of 23 Squadron stand in front of a Gloster Gamecock at Kenley, 1931. They are, from left: Douglas Bader, Harry Day and Geoffrey Stephenson

that he was not only allowed back into the service but was allowed to fly.

Towards the end of November he went to the Central Flying School at Upavon to acquaint himself with modern aircraft types. A brief entry in a 1939 flying magazine announced his return to duty but anyone who read it would never have guessed how this young officer's career was about to blossom. 'Flying Officer D. R. S. Bader, who lost both legs in a flying accident eight years ago, has been accepted again by the RAF as a pilot. Within nine months of his accident he was equipped with two artificial legs and again passed as a first class pilot. Flying Officer Bader applied to be taken back into the Service but was refused. He renewed his application on the outbreak of the War, asking to be allowed to fly single-seaters and has now been accepted,' read the entry.

Soon he was back in a fighter, this time a Spitfire. In February 1940 he went to 19 Squadron at RAF Duxford, then on to 222 Squadron as a flight commander in April.

Like many of his contemporaries, he had read and re-read the many stories of the famous air fighters of World War I, such men as Ball, McCudden and Mannock, and, although the fighter aircraft of 1940 were faster than those of 1917–18, he believed that the fighting tactics and rules learned in those far-off years still held good. He was soon able to put those beliefs into operation. He fought during the battles over the beaches of Dunkirk where, on 1 June 1940, he shot down a Messerschmitt. He was at 3,000 feet when it flew straight in front of him and his first burst blew it out of the sky.

He was then given command of 242 Squadron, a Hurricane unit recently returned from France and mainly consisting of Canadian personnel. They had been through a tough time, having lost practically all their equipment. With his now familiar forcefulness and determination he quickly brought his squadron to operational status, and personally showed the Canadians how he was going to lead them by destroying a Dornier 17 on 11 July. The weather was foul so Bader took off alone to intercept the Dornier, which he eventually found off the Norfolk coast. Ignoring heavy fire from the rear gunner, Bader closed in and opened fire but the bomber entered cloud almost

immediately. Cursing himself for his failure he returned to base, but then came news that the Dornier had in fact crashed into the sea.

Wing fighter tactics

When the Battle of Britain began in earnest, 242 Squadron was ready and, led by Bader, soon made an impression not only on Fighter Command HQ but on the enemy formations they encountered. His squadron was in 12 Group under the control of Air Vice Marshal Trafford Leigh-Mallory, who promoted Bader's idea of a large fighter wing going into action rather than smaller units of only one squadron strength. Whether or not this tactic was wholly correct has often been discussed, but it was Bader who led the Wing (comprising 19, 242 and 310 Squadrons) and they achieved some success.

By the end of the battle, Bader had been credited with more than a dozen personal victories and had received the DSO and DFC. His Canadians had claimed over 60 German raiders. Early in 1941 he became one of the first two wing leaders, commanding the Tangmere Wing, flying Spitfires. In the summer of 1941, the RAF began to take the air war to the enemy over the Channel. Again his

242 Squadron Hurricanes climb to intercept the enemy in late 1940. Under Bader's command, the squadron claimed over 60 victims in the Battle of Britain

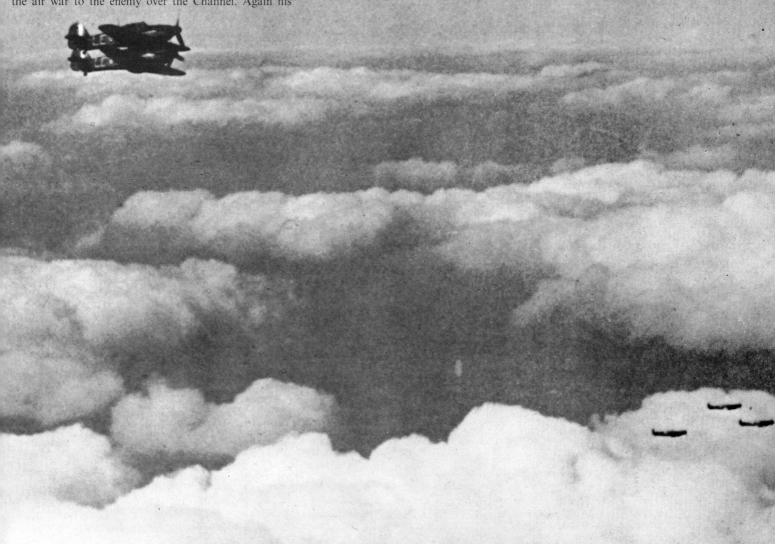

dynamic personality came through as he led his squadrons, Nos. 145, 610 and 616, into the skies over Northern France. Flying 'sweeps' and 'circus' operations, his wing continually engaged enemy Messerschmitts and Bader was always in the thick of the fighting. In June he shot down three Bf 109s and on 2 July destroyed one and probably a second, after which he was awarded a bar to his DSO.

A couple of days later he flamed another Bf 109 near Lille and on the 9 June sent another down to crash near Marzingarbe, then blew up yet another the next day over Chacques. In the first week of July he had netted four Bf 109s destroyed, two probables and two damaged. Bader was on top of his form. Over Hazebrouck on 12 July he set a Bf 109 on fire and shot pieces off three others and a day or so later he went after another but did not fire his guns. Even so, the German pilot baled out, giving Bader a remarkable victory.

Further victories over the RAF's Luftwaffe adversaries came on 19 and 23 July to make a total of eight for the month plus several damaged and others, as Bader insisted on reporting, 'frightened'. Initially Group HQ were not amused when Bader used to report enemy aircraft 'frightened' in his combat reports, but Tangmere Wing had the last laugh after the combat when the German pilot baled out without Bader firing at him. He proudly reported: 'One Bf109 destroyed. Frightened. Confirmed. Seen by two pilots.'

During these months, Bader and his wing, in company with similar wing leaders and fighter wings in Fighter Command's 11 Group, wrote the fighter tactics that were to be carried on over the next two years. Fighter Command, in company with the light bombers of 2 Group, were constantly attacking targets in Northern France, keeping the German fighters engaged. Although today it is known that the RAF did not inflict as much damage on the Luftwaffe as was thought at the time, many lessons were learned which later proved of great value. It also increased the morale of a Britain which had been under attack since July 1940.

However, Bader's part in this campaign was soon to end. On 11 August over Lille the wing tangled with several Bf 109s. After the initial clash he found himself alone but then saw six Bf 109s ahead of him. He slid in behind them and opened fire on the rearmost German which began to leave a trail of flame and fell away. The others did not see their companion go so Bader hammered at another Messerschmitt which poured out white smoke and also went down. This time the other Bf 109s did see him and turned sharply. As he began to bank something hit him: he had collided with a Bf 109. The whole of the fuselage and tail had been sheared off while the rest of the Spitfire, with him in the cockpit, was hurtling earthwards. In trying to get out he found his right leg caught inside the Spitfire as he hung halfway out of the cockpit. Then he was free but minus the offending tin leg. He came to earth in his parachute and was taken prisoner.

Prisoner of war

Bader's war flying was over and three-and-a-half years as a prisoner of war began. For most of this time he was a constant nuisance to his captors. Soon after he received his repaired leg, which the Germans rescued from the wreckage of his Spitfire, he managed to escape from the hospital where he was being kept, but was recaptured. Later, after he received a new leg from England, he was sent to Oflag VIB at Lubeck, where he and two others made a further escape attempt. Then he went to Stalag Luft III at Sagan but again he was so much trouble that finally he was sent to Colditz Castle, where he was to remain until liberated by American troops in 1945.

Back in England he was promoted to Group Captain and given command of the Fighter Leader School at Tangmere. He retired from the RAF on 21 July 1946, returning to Shell Oil to become a senior executive, and was later knighted.

During his 15 months of operations he was officially credited with $22\frac{1}{2}$ German aircraft destroyed, although his own personal tally was 30. Although well known in the RAF by both his combat successes and his forthright leadership, his name really became familiar in the mid 1950s. Paul Brickhill wrote Bader's biography entitled 'Reach for the Sky', which was published in 1954, and two years later a film of the same name was released which put his name and life firmly in the public eye. His courage and determination and his work for the handicapped continue to inspire others.

Target-Britain's Heritage

In 1942 the Luftwaffe launched a series of bombing raids on British cultural centres

The growing menace to German cities, as RAF Bomber Command stepped up their offensive, goaded Hitler into ordering reprisal raids. Incensed in particular by reports of the havoc wrought at the Baltic port of Lübeck late in March 1942, Hitler conveyed his views to his staff, resulting in specific instructions from his Headquarters to Commander-in-Chief Luftwaffe on 14 April. A translation of this teletyped order reads: 'The Führer has decreed that air warfare against England is to be given a more aggressive stamp. When targets are being selected, preference is to be given to those where attacks are likely to have the greatest effect on civilian life. Besides raids on ports and industry, terror attacks of a retaliatory nature are to be carried out against towns other than London. Mining operations may be scaled down to effect these attacks.'

The instruction was passed on to Luftflotte 3, the Luftwaffe Command in the West, consisting mainly of anti-shipping units and Bomber Reserve Training Units, the equivalent of the RAF's Operational Training Units. Nightly sporadic raids were being made over Britain, but activity had been at low key since April 1941 when the nightly blitz, that had followed the Battle of Britain, eased off as Luftwaffe units left for the Eastern Front in preparation for the attack on Russia. To organise the new spate of attacks KG 100, the first German pathfinder unit, was brought back to France to arrange the navigational aids for target finding.

The first of the retaliatory attacks was by about 45

An unexploded bomb is removed from its resting place. Bomb disposal teams, drawn from all three services, played a vital role in speeding the progress of salvage and repair work after the raids

aircraft against the cathedral town of Exeter on the night of 23/24 April. In spite of the River Exe pointing the way inland in the moonlight, the attack was far from concentrated and so it was repeated the following night by about 60 aircraft, causing greater damage; but Exeter's most devastating attack was yet to come.

The target on the night of 25/26 April was the most celebrated of English spas, Bath, although some aircraft dropped their bombs on Bristol. The attack was made in two waves permitting some of the 80 aircraft participating to make two sorties. The aircraft were drawn mainly from KG 2, supplemented by the anti-shipping and training units, involving Do 217s, He 111s and Ju 88s, all controlled from a radio station near Chartres. The moon was still waxing and its reflections on the curving River Avon bounded the target area. This raid affected the majority of the townspeople for, apart from actual hits in residential areas, the bowl of hills in which the town nestled amplified the effect of the blast, shattering windows over a wide area. Three gas holders were extensively damaged, leaving the town without gas for a fortnight. Rescue work was delayed by a hit on the Civil Defence Control Centre and unexploded bombs, as well as flooding by broken water mains, hampered salvage and repair work. To add to the general confusion the town was attacked again the following night, but this second attack was on a reduced scale.

More actual war damage was done in Bath in these two nights than in any other town during the reprisal raids. In the early hours of the 26th there was a direct hit by a high-explosive bomb on the tank gun assembly shop of Stothert & Pitt Ltd at Bridge Road. Almost simultaneously the same company's Lower Bristol Road works, producing gun mountings and minesweeping gear, was hit; the firm's main offices were gutted and the drawing office extensively damaged. The Horstmann Gear Company, making fire control instruments and torpedo parts, had both their plants damaged by high explosive, and unexploded bombs

caused all work to be temporarily suspended. Bath Aircraft Ltd, making components, had their buildings classified 95 per cent destroyed and the Bath works of British Overseas Airways Corporation, engaged on propeller repairs, had their works completely destroyed necessitating dispersal to Pucklechurch. Added to this destruction by high explosive, timber mills engaged on producing ammunition cases were set ablaze.

It was at this time that the series of attacks became to be known as the Baedeker raids. Dr Goebbels, the German Minister for Propaganda related, after a meeting with his Führer, that Hitler averred that there was no other way of bringing the English to their senses; centres of culture, health resorts and civilian centres must be attacked, especially those with few defences, and that they should be repeated until the English tired of terror attacks. Putting part of this discussion in a speech to the German peoples on 26 April, Hitler spoke of taking Baedeker's guides and marking each city off as it was destroyed. It was a name familiar on both sides of the Channel. The British publishing house of John Murray had been printing the guide books of the German publisher Karl Baedeker (1801–59) for over a hundred years. Of the Baedeker aspect of the Bath attack, the most serious loss was the famous Assembly Rooms, gutted by fire, which were not restored for twenty years, and many fine Regency houses that could not be replaced.

A switch to eastern England

Next night there was a switch to eastern England with the cathedral town of Norwich the target for bombers of KG 2 controlled from a radio station near Schipol which plotted courses and advised positions. The control proved inefficient, however, as the bombs, mainly incendiaries, were widely scattered in country areas. The few bombs that fell in the city caused fires which raged due to an acute shortage of water.

On the sixth consecutive night of the raids, the cathedral town of York was the target. This time the proportion of incendiary bombs was even higher and clusters falling north and south of the Minster practically engulfed it in flames, but without causing serious damage to the structure. Some crews concentrated on the railway complex outside the city and part of the London & North Eastern Railway carriage and wagon works, then engaged in making aircraft components, had to be evacuated owing to unexploded bombs.

In the morning, the Luftwaffe sent a single high-flying Ju 86 on a photographic reconnaissance mission over England. Plotted by the RAF and the Royal Observer Corps, it made a course, as expected, over Exeter, Bristol and Bath and then turned north-eastward to York. But instead of turning back as expected, it continued over flying Scarborough and Whitby, the latter a popular resort and a town with a famous abbey. British intelligence assumed this was target photo-mapping as well as collecting evidence of earlier raids and the north-eastern defences were warned. But the night brought another attack on Norwich, in which 45 of the 75 bombers participating scored hits in the town area causing considerable damage and casualties.

Then, after seven consecutive nights of Baedeker-type target attacks, there was a respite. This was partly due to poorer weather and a need for the Luftwaffe to assess their offensive. Exeter, it was seen from photography, had escaped relatively lightly and a further attack was planned. The British were similarly assessing the situation. A redeployment of the anti-aircraft defences involved the re-siting of 252 heavy AA guns to 28 hitherto undefended places. The university towns of Oxford and Cambridge were thought likely targets, and particularly the cathedral town of Ely and Lincoln, which were also recreation towns for the very crews engaged in wrecking German cities. Norwich was thought particularly vulnerable by aircraft approaching over the North Sea and a new balloon barrage was instituted.

Improved defences

The air defences had not been very effective. Eight enemy bombers had been brought down by night fighters, one by AA guns and another fell on British soil for reasons unknown. Additionally Fighter Command had been intruding over France and the Low Countries at night, paying particular attention to airfields. Apart from aircraft damaged on the ground, which could not be assessed, two encountered in the air had been shot down and a Do 217 spotted by a Hurricane pilot as it came in to land at Dinard after the second Norwich attack was shot up and left in flames.

The Luftwaffe returned to the attack on the night of 3/4 May, sending 60 aircraft drawn from various gruppen of KG 2, 30, 55, 77 and 100 to bomb Exeter. This time the town was hard hit. The Gas Light & Coke Company, situated at the Basin, were badly affected; two gas holders were seriously damaged and the coke handling plant was wrecked, while fires raged in nearby oil and liquor stores. The town was the centre of an aircraft repair complex with about 20 works and garages engaged on contract work for Air Service Training Ltd. The Devon Garage, recently expanded for war work, had its new sections put out of commission. The Bedford Garage in Catherine Street, slightly damaged in earlier raids, was gutted, but

Below left: a mainstay of the German bomber force, the Heinkel He 111 was also used by KG100 'pathfinder unit' for target marking over Britain.
Below centre: Canterbury was a prime target for the Luftwaffe both during and after the period of the Baedeker raids.
Below: the Junkers Ju 88, a fast, dependable bomber, outbound for a night attack

Dornier 217 medium bombers of the Luftwaffe at dispersal. A development of the earlier Do17, the Do 217 was a familiar sight over Britain's historic cities in 1942

the aircraft wings being worked upon were salvaged. In Sidwell Street the Cox Bros garage holding 20 fuselages was gutted and the Eveleigh Garage factory was a complete loss.

But this time the defences were more successful. An hour after midnight a Beaufighter pilot spotted a Ju 88 flying at 7,000 feet over the town, so slowly that he was forced to put flaps down and weave to achieve a firing position from astern. After two bursts of cannon-fire the Junkers burst into flames. Later at 9,000 feet, the same pilot saw three enemy bombers flying in a loose 'V' formation – unusual at night but possible because of the bright moonlight that had illuminated the city. A running fight resulted in the fall of another bomber; altogether, Beaufighter crews claimed five that night. At the same time nine Hurricanes, four Havocs and two Bostons were out strafing enemy airfields on the continent.

Evidence brought back to France by a Luftwaffe reconnaissance aircraft next morning showed the cathedral apparently intact surrounded by ruins. There was in fact serious damage to the nave, three bays of the south choir aisle, the sacristy and St James's Chapel, and much that had graced the environs had suffered. The abbot's lodge and the choristers' school were destroyed and part of the bishop's palace was damaged. Streets and alleys of houses, some dating back to medieval times, were reduced to heaps of rubble.

It is a moot point whether or not the raid by 80 aircraft on Cowes the following night, 4/5 May, can be considered a true Baedeker raid. Certainly the town appeared in guide books as a yachting centre, but it was also an industrial seaport and factories and shipyards did suffer considerable damage. Four nights later Norwich was again attacked, but only about half the enemy aircraft operating over East Anglia made the county town of Norfolk their target. There were signs that the Luftwaffe was reverting to their pre-Baedeker tactics; but then the first of the RAF's 1,000-bomber raids, made on Cologne the night of 30 May, brought further retaliatory attacks. Canterbury was subjected to a short but sharp attack on

the night of 31 May. This was followed by a heavier raid on the night of 2 June, when Fighter Command claimed three successes by a Beaufighter, Havoc and Hurricane IIC bringing down two Do 217s and an He 111.

Switch to military targets

Once again the Luftwaffe reverted to military targets in various parts of the United Kingdom and Norwich took its turn on the night of 26 June. Thirty aircraft drawn from 7/KG 100, KG 2 and KGr 106 dropped mainly incendiary bombs. Then on the night of 1 August an incendiary attack by 20 aircraft of KG 2 started 38 fires, but only two people were killed in the fires.

Later in the year two raids on Canterbury caused heavy damage. Events, in time, often become telescoped in peoples' minds and this later ordeal of the city's is often linked with the earlier Baedeker raids – actually they occurred in the period of 'hit and run' raids. On the afternoon of 31 October 30 Fw 190 and Bf 109 fighter-bombers, escorted by fighters of similar types, dropped about twenty high-explosive bombs on Canterbury's shopping centre, residential districts and the electric power station. This was followed by a night attack by 20 bombers making a landfall at North England and setting course for Canterbury. One Do 217 was intercepted by a Beaufighter over the town and was shot down just west of the built-up area; another sighted nearby was chased back and shot down in the Channel a mile off Folkestone.

Canterbury cathedral had sustained superficial damage, but the Chapter Library had been blown to pieces. As with other cathedrals, the main structure remained, the skyline had not been altered. The losses sustained by the Luftwaffe in direct action and accidents were not justified by the damage inflicted on British morale; indeed, the will to win had been strengthened. The so-called Baedeker raids were over, but the 'hit-and-run' raids continued.

Now guide books in describing Bath, Canterbury, Exeter, Norwich and York usually make some reference to damage by air action during World War II; thus Baedeker raids find their place in Baedekers.

Leader of the Air Armada

Italo Balbo was the pioneer of long-range flights by large formations of aeroplanes

During the years following World War I the Italian air force was in the forefront of world aviation and one of its foremost leaders was Italo Balbo. His energy, drive and imagination had recommended him to the Italian leader Mussolini and Balbo was under-secretary of state for air by 1928. The young general, with his trim beard, was an attractive personality and following his leadership of 'Air Armadas' in flights across the North and South Atlantic he became a popular public figure.

In 1925 Savoia-Marchetti had produced a military flying boat with twin engines in tandem above the wing and twin hulls. This aircraft was very sturdy and its performance was steadily improved with the fitting of more powerful engines. The SM55A, fitted with 700hp Fiat engines, was chosen by Balbo to form his first 'Armada' and 14 machines set out in December 1930 to fly from Orbetello, Italy to Rio de Janeiro, Brazil.

These aircraft were to fly in formation and no such thing had been attempted over such a distance before by so

many machines. In fact it is doubtful if any other air force other than the Regia Aeronautica could have done it. Balbo piloted one of the flying boats himself and the journey was not without its disasters. Of the fourteen machines that set out, ten arrived safely having completed the 6,450 miles, but three aircraft were lost and one was unable to finish the flight. In the accidents five airmen were killed, but these fatalities did not deter Balbo. Now air minister, he set about planning another flight, this time across the North Atlantic to Chicago which was holding a 'World's Fair' in 1933.

Organising the 'Armada'

Balbo was a fine administrator and took great pains in organisation of the new 'Armada'. This time a wing of two squadrons, totalling 24 flying boats, was to be used and the aircraft were to be the improved SM55X with two 750hp Isotta-Fraschini Asso engines. Changes included smoother hulls and engine cowlings, fairings over the

Balbo was the first to attempt a long-distance formation flight of this magnitude. The 'Armada', seen here before take-off, was the forerunner of the massed bomber formations of World War II

Following the formation's triumphant return to Rome, Balbo was made the first Marshal of the Italian Air Force. He was later to die at the hands of his own gunners in a tragic wartime accident

joints of all major components and three bladed propellors fitted with spinners.

Balbo also realised the importance of radio for communication between aircraft and also between his 'Armada' and the special radio station that had been set up along the route. Six deep-sea trawlers were also each given an area to cover, so that they might transmit up-to-the-minute weather reports.

The wing was divided up into flights of three aircraft, with a distinctive colour allocated to every two flights (black, red, white and green). To differentiate between the flights with the same colour, one would carry a star marking on the vertical fins and the other would carry a circle, again painted in the flight colour. The leader had one star or circle, the machine on his left three and the machine on his right two markings. The overall finish of the aircraft was silver, but the trimmings were picked out in the flight colour. Each aircraft was given a civil marking relating to the pilot's name. Balbo's was I-BALB and General Pelligrini's was I-PELL.

On Saturday 1 July, the flying-boats took off from Orbetello. Following the plan to keep near water as much as possible while flying overland, so as to have an emergency landing place, they passed over Lake Maggiore and Lake Como before crossing the Alps and reaching the Rhine near Basle. They flew on up the Rhine to Amsterdam, their first stop. Weather conditions were so bad that, by the time the Dutch frontier was reached, they had been forced to fly at a height of only 800 ft.

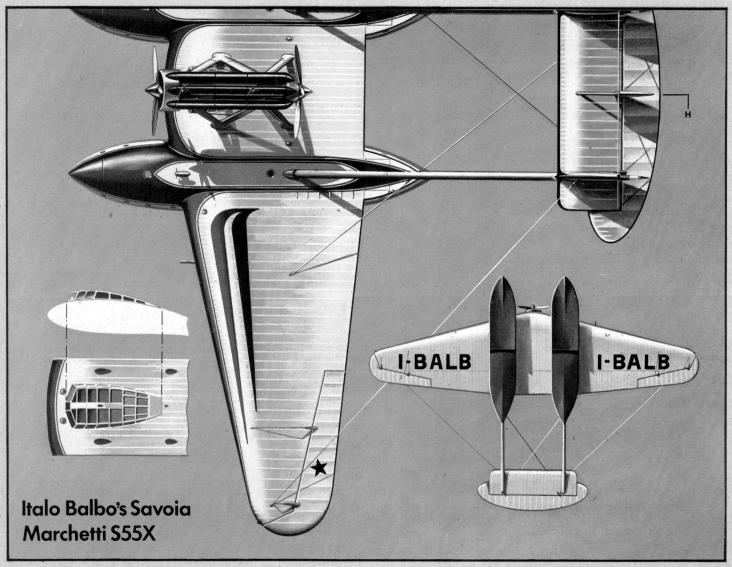

Italo Balbo's Savoia Marchetti S55X

I-BALB I-BALB

All the aircraft touched down at Schellingwoude, the seaplane station on the Zuider Zee near Amsterdam, but then disaster struck. One flying-boat partially capsized in shallow water burying, the bows of the hulls in the mud and flooding the fuselage. All the occupants were slightly hurt and one mechanic was drowned. A reserve machine took the place of the damaged aircraft when the wing took off next morning for Londonderry in Northern Ireland. Having flown in rain storms up the North Sea, the aircraft crossed Scotland between the Firth of Forth and Firth of Clyde and were escorted by Supermarine Southampton flying boats of the Royal Air Force.

Hazardous weather

The flying-boats were delayed for two days by bad weather reports on the route to Reykjavik, Iceland. When the Savoia-Marchettis at last took off they found conditions not greatly improved, being forced to fly on instruments through thick banks of fog. This was a highly dangerous procedure for such a large number of aircraft flying so close together. All the difficulties were overcome and the twenty-four machines landed safely after six hours flying during the 940 mile journey.

The next stop was to be Cartwright on the Labrador coast and it was the longest leg (1,500 miles) of the whole flight. Weather conditions again delayed take-off and the first attempt was cancelled when Balbo's own aircraft failed to get airborne. It was the following Wednesday evening that the flying-boats eventually reached Cart-wright, having flown once more at a height of only a few hundred feet over the cold North Atlantic, which was speckled with icebergs.

Time for the goodwill visit to the World's Fair was now running out and, the flying-boats having been refuelled and the mechanics having checked the engines, the Armada was airborne first thing the next morning for Shediac Bay, New Brunswick. This destination was reached in very good time, due to an assisting tail wind. Hundreds of Canadians gave the Italians a foretaste of the welcomes to come and every assistance was given to set the machines on their way up the St Lawrence to Montreal, where enormous crowds lined the river banks to greet their arrival. This was marred by the behaviour of small boats, which endangered the aircraft and themselves by getting too near the machines' touchdown point.

Acclaimed by Chicago

The 'Armada' took off next morning for Chicago, even though the weather report was not good, because of earlier delays. Storms forced Balbo to change course several times over lakes Erie and Ontario. The weather cleared as they reached Lake Michigan, which was fortunate as many service and private aircraft were waiting to escort them in triumph to their landing place. The flight of 6,065 miles had been achieved in a time of just over forty-eight flying hours. Having been *fêted* by the people of Chicago and visitors to the World's Fair, the Italians now flew to New York, where an even more enthusiastic

Balbo's 'Armada' approaches Amsterdam, first stop on the outward journey. Adverse weather conditions made formation flying hazardous, but ten of the fourteen Isotta-Fraschini engined Savoia-Marchetti flying-boats completed the crossing without incident

The air fleet lie at anchor on Lake Michigan after the outward crossing. Behind them is Chicago, site of the 'World's Fair', where the crews were warmly received on their arrival

reception awaited them, as many New Yorkers were of Italian origin. After five days, which included luncheon for General Balbo with President Franklin D. Roosevelt, the wing set out once more for Shediac. During the flight two machines were forced to drop out due to engine trouble. One landed at Rockland, Maine and the other at St John New Brunswick, but good work by their crews got the aircraft airborne again. They rejoined the main formation in time for the next stage of the return journey, which was to Shoal Harbour, Newfoundland. One flying-boat was forced to land at Cape Traverse, Prince Edward Island, but it was airborne again the next day and reached Shoal Harbour less than twenty-four hours behind the other twenty-three aircraft.

Weather conditions over the North Atlantic now became very bad and the 'Armada' was held up for over a week. The original intention had been to make the next stopping point Valentia, Ireland. However, as the weather showed no signs of improvement, Balbo reluctantly decided that he must change his plans and take a southerly route via the Azores. Due to this upset, it was not until the 8 August that the formation eventually left Shoal Harbour. Two separate landing places had been chosen and, eleven hours after take off, the Wing split up. Nine machines flew to Horta and the remaining fifteen led by Balbo himself touching down at Ponta Delgada, capital of Sao Miguel Island. The reception of the Italians at both places was such that the remainder of the day was declared a public holiday. At Ponta Delgada the governor of the Azores gave a dinner in honour of Balbo and his men. The airmen were ready next morning, despite this hospitality, to take off for Lisbon, but now another fatal accident marred the flight, when one of the flying-boats crashed.

The remaining twenty-three Savoias arrived safely off Lisbon, to be escorted into the Tagus by aircraft of the Portugese air force. The recent tragedy brought about a change in plans and there was no celebration following their arrival, though the usual large crowds turned out to watch the flying-boats arrive. Balbo also decided not to fly to Italy via Marseilles, but to wait a further day and fly direct to Ostia, the ancient port of Rome. There was one ceremony before the last stage and that was the presentation of 'Atlantic Wings' to the crews of the flying-boats by their commander.

First Italian air marshal

The flight across Spain and the Mediterranean brought another problem. The hot weather effected the engine temperatures, causing some machines to drop behind the others. However, when the aircraft reached Ostia as the sun went down, they were flying in impeccable formation and were greeted estatically by the waiting crowds as they circled the city before landing. Following the celebrations the next day, which included a march through Rome, Balbo was made the first Marshal of the Italian Air Force.

During the following years Balbo remained a powerful man in the Italian services and, shortly before World War II, he was made Governor of Libya. He was one of the leading exponents of the attempt to convince the Arabs that Mussolini was on the side of Islam against the British. Following Mussolini's declaration of war in 1940, he took command of the Italian forces against the British in the Western Desert. It was when his aircraft was attempting to land at El Adem, during the course of an air raid by the RAF, that Italian gunners shot him down and he was killed. In memory of a gallant airman, the Royal Air Force sent their condolences, but perhaps Balbo's death was a lucky stroke for the small British desert army, as Balbo would without doubt have proved a stiffer opponent than his successor Marshal Graziani.

The Lone Air Fighter

The solitary Albert Ball was one of the greatest British air aces of World War I

Albert Ball was only 20 years old when he died, but during the last two years of his life he became one of the earliest and greatest of Britain's flying heroes to emerge during World War I.

Born in Nottingham on 14 August 1896, the son of an Alderman, he was educated at Trent College. He left school in 1913 and began a small brass-founding and engineering business, but when war was declared, a year later, he at once volunteered for service. Initially he joined the 2/7th Battalion of the Sherwood Foresters as a private and soon became an NCO. In October 1914 he was commissioned. Hoping to go to France more quickly, he transferred to the North Midlands Cycle Corps, but their duties kept them and him in England. It was at this time that his interest turned to flying. He paid for lessons at Hendon and received his licence on 15 October 1915. After that he was attached to the Royal Flying Corps to receive further training and gained his 'wings' on 22 January 1916. Finally his wish to go to the fighting in France was fulfilled and he joined 13 Squadron at Savay.

No. 13 Squadron was a corps general-duties squadron flying two-seat BE2c aeroplanes. Soon Ball was taking his turn at flying reconnaissance sorties and artillery observation missions over the front lines. On 20 March his engine stopped soon after take-off; he crash-landed but both he and his observer were unhurt. On the 27th he was forced down again–this time by enemy gunfire. On occasions he managed to get flights in a single-seat Bristol Scout and found he enjoyed the freedom this little machine gave him. It was a foretaste of things to come. He also had his first clash with enemy aircraft when, on 29 April, he and his observer forced down a hostile plane near Rouvroy.

The Nieuport Scout

On 7 May 1916, a significant date, as will be seen later, he was sent to 11 Squadron, which had a mixture of two-seat FE2b machines and single-seat Nieuport and Bristol Scouts. Ball was given a Nieuport, which suited his individuality, and was soon roaming into the hostile skies over enemy territory, searching for airborne adversaries. During the rest of May he had several fights with enemy aeroplanes, forcing many either to retreat or land–a typical expedient for getting out of trouble in those days.

On 1 June, he circled above the German airfield at Douai as a challenge to its inhabitants. When two German aeroplanes finally took-off to engage him, Ball's aggressive attacks forced both to land again hurriedly.

After a spell of leave, Ball returned to his Nieuport

Below: Ball, second from right, is pictured with fellow pilots of 56 Squadron. On Ball's right is the squadron's commanding officer Major G. A. Bloomfield

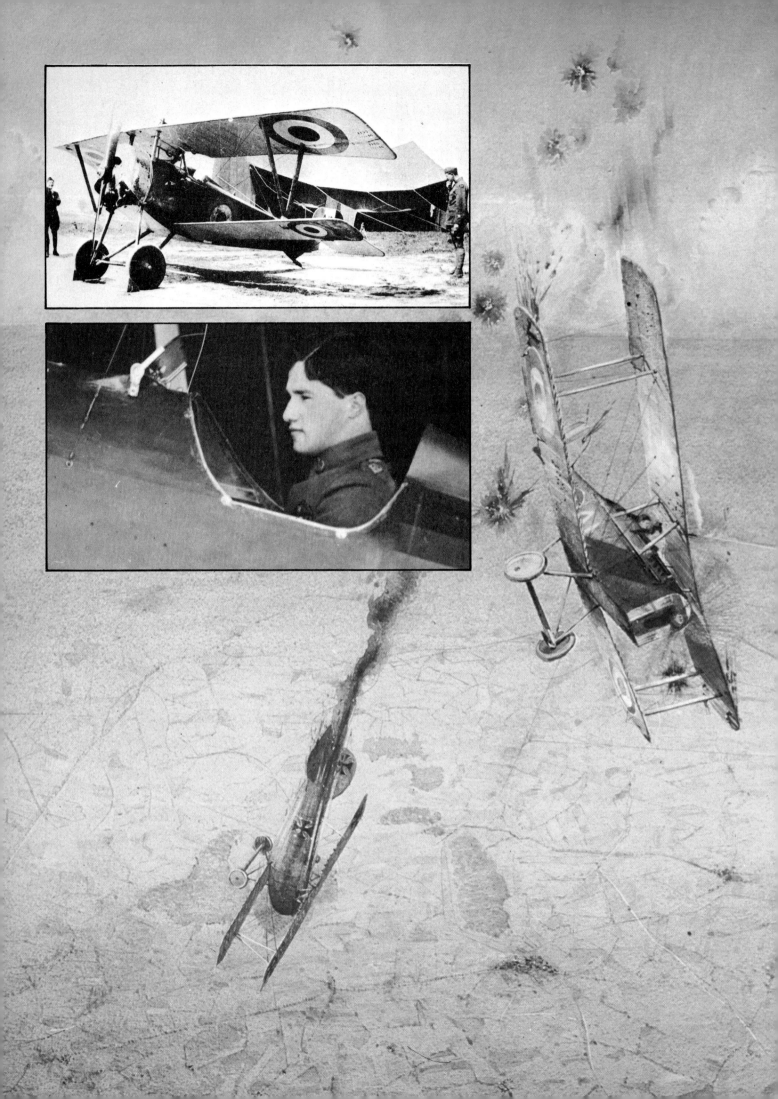

towards the end of June and on the 26th attacked and destroyed a German observation balloon. He soon received the MC for his work. The great Somme offensive began on 1 July and among the many hundreds who died on the ground were men from his old regiment, the Sherwood Foresters. In the air the following day, Ball shot down a Roland two-seater which smashed to pieces near the Mercatel-Arras road. Thirty minutes later he encountered an Aviatik two-seater, which also went down under his fire to crash in a field.

Ball was now feeling the effects of his constant patrols but was annoyed when he was sent to 8 Squadron for a 'rest'. This squadron flew the BE2c, like his former 13 Squadron, and he was unhappy because instead of air fighting, for which he was beginning to acquire a liking, he was back flying bombing sorties and artillery observation flights. On 28 July he took a spy over enemy lines and landed him in occupied territory, but the Frenchman refused to get out and Ball had to fly him home again. Ball was constantly on the offensive, even in a BE, and he was thus eventually sent back to 11 Squadron on 10 August.

Flight Commander

Seated once again in the cockpit of his favourite machine, the Nieuport 17 Scout, Ball began an aggressive run of active flying over the front. He forced down two Rolands on 17 August, while on the 22nd he crashed another Roland, sent a second down in flames and then forced a third to land. The next day he was posted to 60 Squadron under the command of Major R. Smith-Barry, where, because of his recent 'lone-wolf' activities, he was allowed to fly when and where he pleased. By the end of the month he had added two aircraft destroyed to his rising score of victories, in addition to forcing four more to land. He then went on leave again, returning on 11 September, this time to take command of A Flight of 60 Squadron. Although now responsible for a flight, he continued to fly alone whenever possible, for this was how he fought best.

Ball began a fantastic fortnight of air fighting, starting with the destruction of two Rolands on 15 September. Two more were destroyed on the 21st, when another was forced to land. The next day he came up against a Fokker DI scout which crashed after a brief dog-fight. On the 23rd he destroyed an Albatros DII and the next morning he was out looking for more trouble. At 05.45 Ball, against orders, fired at some balloons in order to attract the attention of any enemy machines that might be around. Three Albatros Scouts soon appeared and Ball quickly attacked, hitting one from underneath at fifteen yards range, whereupon the German spun down to crash near Haplincourt. Two mornings later he fought another Albatros single-seater above Bapaume. Getting below his adversary, he pulled down his wing-mounted Lewis gun and fired up into the German aeroplane, which im-

The SE5 in which Ball was to die some two months later, pictured at London Colney, then 56 Squadron's base, about March 1917

mediately burst into flames. That evening he fought a formation of eight Roland two-seaters near Graincourt, firing a whole double drum of ammunition from his Lewis into the underside of one, which went spinning earthwards. He was so hotly engaged, however, that he could not see whether or not it crashed.

During September Ball received the Distinguished Service Order and Bar, together with the Russian Order of St George. His scoring continued on 1 October, when he forced three single-seaters to land. Three days later he was sent home to England for a rest, going to 34 Reserve Squadron at Orfordness as an instructor. During his periods at the front he had destroyed 12 German machines and one balloon, sent another aeroplane down 'out of control' and had forced a further 19 to Land. In November he received a second Bar to his DSO.

A month of victories

In England, and especially in his home town, Ball was very much the hero; Nottingham made him a Freeman of the City. Yet he continued to press for a return to active duty in France. Eventually, in February 1917, he was sent to London Colney, Hertfordshire, where 56 Squadron was forming and he became commander of A Flight. The squadron was equipped with the new SE5, which Ball did not like as much as the Nieuport. In fact, when 56 went to France on 7 April Ball managed to acquire a Nieuport, which he flew whenever possible.

No. 56 Squadron was to become one of the most famous fighter squadrons of World War I. In exactly one month Ball ran up an incredible fourteen victories, starting with three kills on 23 April – the squadron's first victories. Two more victories came to him on the 26th and another 'double' on the 28th. Leading two of his flight on the evening of 1 May he encountered six Albatros two-seaters near Marquion at 15,000 ft. Diving down in his SE5 he gained his favourite underneath position by zooming up under his opponent and opened fire with the wing-mounted Lewis gun. The two-seater dived, with Ball close behind firing his fuselage mounted Vickers gun until the Albatros went into the ground.

The next day he destroyed an Albatros DIII and sent a two-seater spinning earthwards. On 4 May, his guns claimed another Albatros Scout. The following evening

Ball was leading his flight when they engaged two enemy scouts. Ball attacked one and drove it down before the second one attacked him. He climbed and, as he came out of a loop, found the German attacking him from head-on. Both fighters blazed away at each other as the gap between them narrowed and both were hit. Ball's SE5 was struck in the oil tank, which showered oil back over him. He landed safely, but the German had been seriously damaged and crashed. Two more single-seat Albatros scouts fell under his guns on the 5th and his final victim, another Albatros, was destroyed on the evening of the 6th, near Sancourt, while he was flying his personal Nieuport.

The last flight

Ball's life ended on 7 May 1917, exactly one year after his posting to 11 Squadron in 1916 to be a scout pilot. A certain amount of mystery still surrounds Ball's death, for nobody actually saw him go down. During confused fighting in the evening sky between Cambrai and Douai, he was last seen chasing an enemy aeroplane towards some clouds and later that day, a stunned 56 Squadron finally realised that Ball was missing. The Germans buried him with full military honours at Annoeulin cemetery on 9 May 1917.

Ball had destroyed 23 German aircraft, sent two German aeroplanes down 'out of control' and forced 21 to land, a total of 47 combat victories. On 8 June 1917 the London Gazette announced that Ball had been awarded the Victoria Cross. The citation to the award stated 44 victories but when he presented Ball's father, Sir Albert Ball, with the coveted decoration at Buckingham Palace on 21 July, the King confirmed to him that his son had accounted for 47 of the enemy.

Ball had achieved all this by early 1917, when air fighting was still comparatively new and tactics were still being evolved. He had taught himself the ways of the air fighter and his bold, 'attack-everything' doctrine and aggressive actions had established him as Britain's first great air ace. Yet his own ways were simple. He liked to fly alone, to be the hunter and stalk his prey, but rarely did he turn away when faced with uneven odds. On the ground, too, he was more often than not on his own, tending his little garden on the edge of the airfield or playing his violin in the small hut which he built himself.

Flying Cavalryman

Francesco Baracca was Italy's top-scoring fighter pilot in World War I

The man who was destined to become Italy's leading fighter pilot of World War I was born on 9 May 1888, at Lugo di Romagna, just outside Ravenna. As a young man, Francesco Baracca soon decided upon a military career when his schooling in Florence was completed. Although it was against his parents' wishes, Baracca enrolled in the Military Acadamy at Modena in 1907, choosing to join the cavalry. He completed his training and was sent to join the 2nd Cavalry Regiment.

In 1912 he decided to learn to fly and trained in France, where, under an agreement with the French, Italian pilots received their initial flight training. He passed all his tests in July and returned to Italy as a fully qualified pilot. Over the next two years he added greatly to his flying experience, which was to prove valuable when war came.

Italy was neutral at the beginning of World War I, but in May 1915 she declared war on Austria. By this time Baracca was a proficient single-seat pilot, but his first war patrols were flown in a Nieuport two-seater over the Udine front in Northern Italy. During the late summer he had his first encounters with Austrian aeroplanes. He then went on to single-seat Nieuport 11s and leading a patrol

of 70ª Squadriglia at dawn on 7 April 1916, attacked an Austrian Aviatik two-seater which he forced down inside the Italian lines. In the tradition of the early period of the war, Baracca landed nearby and greeted his victims.

His second victory was achieved on 16 May. Fourteen Austrian machines flew over to bomb Italian positions and Baracca, who had only just awoken, was among those who took off to intercept them. Three Austrians were brought down by the squadriglia, Baracca's victim falling at Gorizia. It was not all air fighting, however: Baracca and his comrades were often engaged in low level strafing attacks on Austrian trench positions.

Prancing horse insignia
Another aeroplane fell under his attacks on 23 August, this one going down in flames; his fourth victory came on 16 September and his fifth, an Albatros two-seater, was

Above: Baracca's personal 'prancing horse' insignia, which his aircraft bore from late 1916 onwards.
Below: Major Baracca pictured with one of his last victims, an Albatros D.III, which he forced down in June 1918

propeller, wings, petrol tank (which fortunately did not catch fire) and engine, the latter stopping dead, causing him to force-land near Cividale, but his second opponent also fell, crashing near Matajur.

On the ground below, the Italian Army was in full retreat following the disastrous battle of Caporetto. Baracca's men had to pack up and move to Pordenone, but they were able to change to the better SPAD SXIIIs. They certainly needed the improved version of the SPAD, as they now had to contend with Godwin Bromowski and his Austrian squadron of red-painted Albatros Scouts.

Baracca, however, was still able to make his presence felt and sent down two more two-seaters on 6 November. By the end of the year he had brought his score to 30. He was then taken away from active flying at the front, and sent to the Ansaldo aeroplane factory at Torino to help with the development and testing of the new fighter aeroplanes being built there.

Later in the new year he returned to his squadriglia and in March moved with it to Treviso. He also received Italy's highest award, the Medaglia d'Oro al Valor Militare

forced down near Tolmezzo on 25 November. It was at this time that he embellished his Nieuport with the crest which was to become famous, the green 'prancing horse' insignia, remeniscent of his cavalry service.

He began the new year of 1917 by destroying an Albatros two-seater on New Year's Day and by early May had brought his score to ten. These were his last claims while flying the Nieuport Scout because a flight from 70ª Squadriglia was detached to become the nucleus of a new squadriglia, No. 91ª, and Baracca was to lead one of the unit's flights. It also meant a change of aeroplane, as this new squadriglia was equipped with the French SPAD SVII, on to one of which Baracca again painted his personal insignia.

Baracca did not take long to bring success to the new squadriglia: he shot down an Albatros over Castel de Monte on 13 May and a week later crashed another near Plava. He sent another Albatros down in flames between the lines on 3 June, and was then given command of the squadriglia, the unit moving to Istrana. Leading 91ª, he gained his 14th victory on 7 July and by the end of September he had 19 confirmed 'kills'.

He scored his first double victory on 21 October above San Gabriele. Engaging five single-seat Albatros DIIIs, which seemed intent on his destruction, he successfully outfought them, then attacked a brace of two-seaters, shooting both down.

Intensified air war

The air war over Northern Italy intensified towards the end of 1917, as evidenced on 25 October, when Baracca's squadriglia shot down six Austrians during several dog-fights for the loss of two pilots, his own SPAD being badly shot up during one encounter. He survived – although one of his attackers did not.

The Italian was out early the following morning and found two German Aviatik two-seaters. The first went down following Baracca's attack but the second put up a slightly better, if futile, defence, putting several bullets through the SPAD. Bullet holes were later located in its

Apparecchi Newport pronti per partire

at a special ceremony at La Scala opera house in Milan. It was a splendid occasion at which two of Baracca's own pilots, Fulco Ruffo and Pier Piccio, both of whom had flown many sorties with him and had also recently spent time flight testing at Torino, were also decorated with this coveted medal.

Battle of the Piave

On 3 May 1918, Baracca gained his 31st victory when he fought six Albatros DIII Scouts, destroying one. On the 22nd he and Sergente d'Urso shot down one of six reconnaissance machines they found over the front, the machine falling near Borgo Malanotte. Flying with Sergente Aliperta on 15 June, Baracca attacked an Albatros they saw bombing Italian troops at Montello and fifteen minutes later he spotted more enemy aircraft. This was the first day of the Battle of the Piave and it was important to keep the air clear of enemy aircraft. He saw the enemy over San Biagio—a single two-seater reconnaissance machine escorted by no fewer than two dozen single-seater scouts. It was obviously an important observation patrol by the Austrians and Baracca's duty was to stop it doing its work and if possible prevent it from returning home with information. Ignoring the strong fighter escort, Baracca nosed over in his SPAD and dived full out, right through the escort and, firing from close range, sent the two-seater down. It was his 34th and final victory.

With the Piave River battle still raging, orders came on 19 June for the 91ª Squadriglia to make a low flying sortie along the front and harass and attack enemy troops and positions. The SPADS took off shortly after 1830 hours led by the commander and, flying along the front, continually dived to strafe enemy positions. They met heavy return fire and lost sight of their leader in the smoke and confusion over the battle area. They later returned alone and had to report that they had not seen Baracca during the last attacks. It was discovered later that he had been hit in the forehead by a single bullet and killed instantly. His SPAD had crashed and Baracca thrown clear. His body was not discovered until after the Austrian retreat, when it was found lying close to the River Piave, above which Baracca had flown his last mission.

Left: the certificate of qualification which authorised Baracca to fly the Nieuport Scout. Below left and bottom: a feature of the Nieuport, which Baracca flew until early 1917, was its half-chord lower wing, giving the type a 'sesquiplane' or '1½ wing' configuration. Armament consisted of a Lewis gun above the wing

Left: most of the Italian-flown Nieuports were licence-built by Macchi. A mechanic spins the propeller of a Nieuport in Northern Italy. Below left: a SPAD, bearing the famous 'prancing horse'. Baracca led 91ª Squadriglia, which flew this type, from May 1917 until his death on 19 June 1918

The Canadian hero

The pugnacious airman who would not be kept out of action for long

Right: Lt Col W. G. Barker after the award of the Victoria Cross in 1918. The RAF retained the Army style of rank designation until 1919

'Billy' Barker was born in Dauphin, Manitoba, Canada, on 3 November 1894. When war came in 1914 he joined the Canadian Mounted Rifles and with them went to England and then to France. Life in the trenches did not impress him overmuch and he soon decided to leave the mud of Flanders for the cleaner air above.

William George Barker, to give him his full name, volunteered to become an observer in the Royal Flying Corps and was sent to 9 Squadron flying BE 2c machines. receiving a commission in April 1916. With his observers

Billy Barker pictured in April 1919 with a captured Fokker D.VII at Hounslow Aerodrome near London. The D.VII was generally acknowledged to be one of the leading fighter aircraft of World War I

Lewis gun, he drove down a Roland two-seater on 29 July for his first victory.

After service with 9 Squadron, he also flew with both 4 and 15 Squadrons and was awarded the Military Cross. Selected for pilot training, Barker returned to 15 Squadron after gaining his 'wings'. The unit was now flying two-seater RE 8s. In this type he shot down a Fokker scout on 25 March 1917 which was seen to crash. Later in 1917, having won a bar to his MC, he was posted home to England to become an instructor. However, he proved such a nuisance by continually requesting more active duty that early in October he was sent to 28 Squadron, which was preparing for overseas duty. He was given

command of a flight and went to France with the new squadron almost immediately.

His prowess as a fighting pilot soon showed, for by the end of that first month in France he had shot down at least five German aeroplanes. In November, 28 Squadron was one of the British units sent to Italy to assist the Italians, following their defeat at Caporetto, and it was in Italian skies that Barker really excelled.

Italian Front

He claimed his first victory on this new front on 29 November when he destroyed an Albatros Scout. During December he got another and flamed two observation

balloons, then began the new year by destroying another Albatros on 1 January. The award of the Distinguished Service Order came later that month. He was almost continually on the offensive during these first weeks of 1918 and by the end of March had accounted for ten aeroplanes and nine balloons, five of the latter being destroyed in company with another pilot during one raid on enemy positions on 12 February. In April he was given command of one of the other Sopwith Camel units in Italy, 66 Squadron.

Still in the familiar seat of his personal Sopwith Camel, B6313, in which he was to gain all his Italian victories and which he brought with him from 28 Squadron, he led his squadron in the air, always heading patrols or even flying out alone in order to fight his Austrian and German opponents. Between 17 April and 13 July, mostly while the Battle of the Piave raged, he shot down sixteen hostile aircraft, all but two being scouts. He was awarded a second bar to his Military Cross and the Italian Silver Medal for Valour.

Barker was then given command of 139 Squadron, which flew two-seater Bristol Fighters, but he insisted on bringing his Camel with him. Although he flew several sorties in the Bristols, he often flew his Camel and gained a further six victories with it, four enemy aircraft being destroyed plus a further two driven down 'out of control'.

Top: Barker's Camel, serialled B6313, which was the highest scoring Camel of the war. It was scrapped when he left Italy in September 1917.
Above: Barker flew with 28 Squadron in Italy before taking command of 66 Squadron. He is pictured over Northern Italy in a Camel of 66 Squadron in 1918

On one noteworthy mission he flew at this time, he piloted a tri-motor Caproni behind enemy lines to drop an Italian agent, an action for which he received a second Italian Silver Medal.

Towards the end of September he was posted back to England, but he had to leave his faithful Camel B6313 behind because it was worn out. He had gained nearly 50 victories in this machine. It was, in fact, the highest scoring Camel of the war and as such should have been preserved, but sadly it was reduced to scrap.

Back in England and the recipient of a bar to his DSO, Barker might well have relaxed and been content to finish the war as an instructor, but he could not be kept out of action for long. At this time, he frequently asked for operational duty but was firmly told to continue as an instructor. Finally, using the argument that he could not possibly train pilots to fight on the Western Front when he had not himself fought in France for almost a year, he was granted an attachment for a few days (taking one of the new Sopwith Snipe aeroplanes) to 201 Squadron in France, which flew Camels. He flew on several patrols over the front, but failed to make contact with the enemy and soon his time in France was at an end.

Epic air battle
On 27 October, he packed his gear, stowed it aboard his Snipe and reluctantly took off to return to England. But he could not resist just one last look at the war front and cruised along near the lines. Then, below, he spotted a lone German two-seater reconnaissance machine, which was just what he was hoping for. He dived down, opened fire and had the satisfaction of seeing it fall earthwards. As he watched, a parachute appeared and, probably

fascinated by this, he failed to see enemy fighters above him. Several Fokkers dived upon the lone Snipe and a burst of fire from one smashed one thigh. He immediately fainted and began to spin down but came to still in the midst of his adversaries and fought back. He shot down one Fokker, was hit again in the other thigh and again fainted. As his machine fell away again, he cleared his head, only to find his enemies still about him, shooting his Snipe to ribbons. In spite of his two painful injuries he put up a terrific fight, blasting two more Fokkers from the sky before being wounded yet again, this time by a bullet in his left elbow.

Now low down, he passed out again but managed to regain consciousness long enough to crash land. In the crash he broke his nose to add to his already severe injuries, but he survived. For several days he lingered between life and death and it was during this period that the announcement was made that he had been awarded the Victoria Cross for his spectacular and heroic air fight. In this he had, in spite of painful wounds, continued to fight and destroy three German fighters in addition to the reconnaissance two-seater.

The war over, he recovered to receive his highly deserved decoration from the King. He ended the war with 52 victories, and was also one of the most highly decorated fighters of the Great War; in addition to his VC, DSO and bar, MC and two bars, he had received the French Légion d'honneur, the Croix de Guerre, and two Italian Silver Medals for Valour.

Return to Canada
He returned to his native Canada and, when his wounds healed, went into partnership with another famous Canadian flyer, Colonel W. A. 'Billy' Bishop VC, DSO, MC, DFC. Together they operated an air charter service from Toronto to Lake Muskoka, Ontario. Later, Barker decided to join the Royal Canadian Air Force, and he returned to England to attend the RAF Staff College at Andover. For a period he became Military Air Attaché in London, but the peacetime air force did not really appeal to him, so he resigned his commission and tried his hand at tobacco farming. However, flying was still in his blood and he went into civil aviation, becoming the Canadian head of an American aeroplane company.

On 12 March 1930, at Rockcliffe, Ottowa, a new Fairchild two-seater was to be test flown and demonstrated and Barker insisted that he would be the pilot. It was thought that as he climbed, the throttle lever slipped and his crippled left elbow prevented him from reaching the lever quickly enough. The machine stalled, and crashed into the Ottowa River. Barker was killed instantly. He was buried in Toronto on 15 March with full military honours as befitted this heroic and colourful flyer.

Above: Barker, with the Prince of Wales (later King Edward VIII) as passenger, takes off in a Bristol F2B Fighter from Villaverla in Italy. At the time Barker was CO of 139 Squadron.
Below: Barker beside a wrecked Sopwith Camel, when he commanded a flight of 28 Squadron early in 1918

Scourge of the Red Air Force

Gerhard Barkhorn shot down more than 300 aircraft in World War II

Born in Königsberg/Ostpreussen on 20 March 1919, Gerhard Barkhorn began his Luftwaffe flying training in 1938. A year later he was piloting Messerschmitt 109s and had begun a six-year association with fighter aircraft which made him the second highest scoring fighter pilot not only of the German Luftwaffe, but also of the world.

By Allied standards, however, Barkhorn was a slow starter. He flew with Jagdgeschwader 2 (JG2) 'Richthofen' during the Battle of Britain before transferring to II/JG52 in August, 1940. It was well into 1941 before he gained his first combat success, by which time JG52 had moved to the Russian Front for Operation Barbarossa, the invasion of Russia in June 1941.

This first kill came on 2 July, on Barkhorn's 120th operational sortie. From then onwards his score of confirmed victories slowly began to rise, though not in the multiple kills which some of the fighter pilots on the Russian Front achieved, but in ones and twos over the next two-and-a-half years. In fact, his highest score on any one day was seven, while his best on one sortie was on 20 July, 1942, when he downed a modest four Russian aircraft. With the front usually so full of Russian aircraft, constantly being engaged by Luftwaffe pilots during several missions per day, it was not uncommon for some pilots to shoot down three or four on each mission. The record for a single mission went to Erich Rudorffe of JG54 who shot down 13 Russians on 6 November 1943, while Emil Lang, of the same unit, claimed 18 in a single day. In one brisk period Lang gained 72 kills in three weeks.

Barkhorn received the coveted Knight's Cross on 23 August 1942, after gaining his 59th victory and on 19 December he downed his 100th Russian aeroplane.

Barkhorn celebrating his 250th victory in the cockpit of his Messerschmitt Bf109 in February 1944. At that time he commanded Jagdgeschwader 52, whose emblem is shown (top)

Geschwader Kommodore

In June 1943 he was promoted and made Kommodore of JG52. He steadily added further victories until his score reached 200 on 30 November. He became the fifth German pilot to gain that number of victories, the other four being Hermann Graf, Hans Philipp, Gunther Rall and Walter Nowotny. It took Barkhorn until 13 February 1944 to notch up his 250th victory, becoming only the third pilot to reach this figure, and was awarded the Swords to his Knight's Cross. It was almost a year before he achieved the magic figure of 300 victories. This was due to many causes, not the least of which were the months spent in hospital recovering from wounds.

One day, in May 1944, Barkhorn led his Bf109s as escort to Stukas, which were headed by the famous tank-busting ace Hans-Ulrich Rudel. This was Barkhorn's sixth escort mission that day and they were on the return flight when their controller warned the Messerschmitt pilots that Russian fighters were near them. At this time Barkhorn had 273 victories and was feeling tired and possibly slightly over-confident. A Russian fighter dived through the German formation and opened fire on the leader, shooting Barkhorn's Bf109 to pieces. He survived but spent the next four months in hospital.

Had it not been for this, Barkhorn may well have been the war's top fighter pilot, for the only flyer to score more victories was his friend and rival Erich Hartmann. When Barkhorn was wounded, Hartmann's personal score was only just over 200 victories.

Escort to an enemy

During Barkhorn's combat career he met almost every type of Russian fighter, including Allied types used by the Red Air Force, such as the Spitfire, Hurricane and American Airacobra. In his own experience the Russian Yak 9 was the best fighter he encountered. His own preference was the Bf109F in which to fly and fight.

Barkhorn was shot down nine times, baled out twice and was wounded twice. Yet he fought with compassion.

Barkhorn with a group of his pilots on the Eastern Front. His score of 301 enemy aircraft destroyed was only surpassed by one other pilot in World War II

On one sortie, after he had crippled a Russian fighter and set it on fire, he flew alongside the burning machine and gestured to the enemy pilot to bale out, which he did. When asked later why he had not finished off his opponent, he remarked: 'You must remember that once that Russian pilot was the baby of a beautiful Russian girl. He has his right to life and love, the same as we do.'

Hartmann passed Barkhorn's score in the summer of 1944 and Barkhorn was among the first pilots to congratulate his young friend on his success. Hartmann went on to score 352 victories and he and Barkhorn became the only two men in World War II to achieve more than 300 kills. Although friendly rivals, they both admired each other as fighter pilots. Barkhorn married in 1943 and when Hartmann was married the following August, Barkhorn was one of the wedding witnesses. Hartmann was not the only admirer of 'Gerd' Barkhorn. Almost every surviving German pilot who knew or served with him readily admitted that he was one of the Luftwaffe's most respected air fighters of World War II.

Jet fighter missions

Barkhorn scored that 300th victory on 5 January 1945 and made only one more kill before he was transferred to command JG6. Soon afterwards he went to JV44, the squadron of experts, to fly the Messerschmitt 262 jet. He only flew two missions in the 262, however, and was shot down on the second. He had been about to attack an American bomber formation when his right-hand jet engine failed. Breaking away, he became a target for American Mustangs. Chasing the 262 down, the Mustangs

gradually caught up with him as he found a place to crash land. He pushed back the cockpit canopy, ready to get out quickly but as he grounded he was jolted upwards and the canopy slid forward, hitting him in the neck. His injury put him in hospital again and the war ended before he returned to combat.

He had flown 1,104 fighter missions during the war and fought numerous combats to achieve his 301 victories. He recalled that his toughest fight was during a scrap in 1943 with a Russian LaGG 3 fighter flown by a pilot in a Russian Guards Squadron. The two pilots fought each other for fully 40 minutes and Barkhorn knew he was up against a good pilot when he saw the red painted nose and cowling of the Russian aeroplane which denoted an elite squadron. Neither pilot could make any impression on the other and finally they called it a draw and each flew his own way home. On landing, Barkhorn was dripping with perspiration and he wondered if his opponent was in a similar state. This, in fact, said much for the Russian pilot, since Gerd was acknowledged by his comrades to be one of the greatest dog-fighters on the Russian Front.

When the war ended, Barkhorn, along with hundreds of others, was imprisoned but fortunately he was in the hands of the Western Powers and did not suffer the years in prison that many of his friends did who were captured by the Russians. In 1955 he joined the New German Air Force and had a refresher course under Royal Air Force tuition at RAF Valley in Wales. He soon became a Colonel and later a General, with the position of Director of Operations at the 4th ATAF at Ramstein. He continued to serve into the mid-1970s.

When more than a quarter of a million people attended the first great international aviation meeting at Reims, France, in August 1909, flying became established as an entertainment, a spectator sport, though with little commercial or military interest. Aviators and aircraft manufacturers were quick to exploit the wave of near-hysterical public enthusiasm which followed, and air meetings blossomed in Europe and America.

Claude Grahame-White, a fine pilot and born showman, promoted regular displays and races at Hendon, near London. A typical advertisement read: 'Racing every Saturday and Holiday. Special exhibition flights every Thursday, Saturday and Sunday afternoon by well-known aviators. Passenger flights from two guineas'. Meanwhile Glen Curtiss, the popular hero of Reims, returned triumphant to Hammondsport, New York, with the James Gordon-Bennett Trophy and his $7,500 prize and immediately set up a school to train exhibition fliers.

Even the conservative Wright brothers, who had never been much given to public display of their skills, began preparing a team of show pilots. Graduates of the two schools toured the country, performing at carnivals, county and state fairs, political rallies, anywhere that might attract paying customers, thus earning for themselves a name originally given to bands of strolling players who set up their theatres in farmers' barns and were therefore known as barnstormers.

Death-defying dive

One of the best and most flamboyant exhibition fliers was Lincoln Beachey, who flew for Curtiss. Beachey's speciality was a 'death-defying' dive, in which he took his Curtiss Pusher biplane up to 4,000 feet, commenced a near vertical dive and pulled out so close to the ground that lady spectators would faint away. He once challenged his contemporaries to a competition: they would all climb to

the same height, shut off their engines and dive for the ground. Whoever pulled out last would be the winner. Not surprisingly, there were no takers. Beachey also staged aeroplane-versus-automobile races, taking on some of the great racing drivers of the day, including Eddie Rickenbacker and Barney Oldfield. Early in 1913 Beachey announced his retirement, declaring that the crowds came only to see him die and that his routine, which 22 other pilots had died trying to copy, served no useful purpose.

There were women barnstormers, too. Matilde Moisant, a schoolmistress, and her friend Harriet Quimby, the pretty drama critic of *Leslie's Weekly* learned to fly in 1911 and flew around America together. Matilde caused much gossip with the divided skirts she wore in the interests of modesty in the draughty open-cockpit of her Blériot named 'Lucky Thirteen', whilst Harriet fluttered

The Curtiss Jenny was the best American trainer of World War I and, because many war-surplus Jennies became available in 1918, the type was a favourite mount of barnstormers in the United States

Avro 504K G-EBIZ, operated by Alan Cobham's Flying Circus in 1932

Dimensions
Span 10·97 m (36 ft)
Length 8·98 m (29 ft 6 in)
Height 3·18 m (10 ft 5 in)

Engine
One Gnome, le Rhône or Clerget rotary

Performance
Maximum speed 145 km/h (90 mph)
Service ceiling 4880 m (16,000 ft)

Opposite top: wing-walking on a Curtiss JN-4D Jenny. Opposite bottom: Lillian Boyer, one of the few female barnstormers. The mortality rate was high; there were 85 deaths and 162 injuries in 1923 alone. Right: Ormer Locklear, the most famous wing-walker of the era, in 'wild west' garb astride a Jenny over Los Angeles. He became a film stunt-pilot and later spun to his death

the hearts of gentlemen in a mauve satin outfit which must have been quite unsuitable for flying. Poor Harriet died during a display at Harvard Field, Boston, when she and her passenger were flung from the aeroplane during a steep dive, and Matilde retired shortly afterwards after a series of disastrous accidents.

Crashes were inevitable, for the aeroplanes were fragile and sadly underpowered. In one year alone, 40 exhibition fliers died, seven of them from the Wright and Curtiss teams. But if the risks were high, so too were the rewards. Louis Blériot received $4,000 for one five-day stint of demonstrations in Berlin. The Wrights paid their pilots $20 a week, all expenses found, plus $50 per flight, in return for any prize money they might win. And win they did; one pilot handed over $250,000 in two years.

Early aerobatics
Such is the fickleness of human nature that the crowds soon tired of the novelty of seeing flying machines merely defying gravity. They wanted more excitement, more daring, more stunts. The first truly aerobatic manoeuvre was not performed by an exhibition flier, but by a young Imperial Russian Air Service lieutenant, Peter Nesterov,

who looped his 70 hp Nieuport IV monoplane over Syretzk Aerodrome, near Kiev, in August 1913, and was promptly banished to the guardhouse for what his superiors called 'useless audacity'.

Audacious it certainly was, but not useless, for the exhibition fliers quickly began experimenting with more advanced aerobatics. Adolphe Pégoud, a *protégé* of Blériot's school at Buc, near Paris, performed loops, 'side-somersaults' (rolls), vertical 'S' figures, tailslides and steep sideslips, modest enough manoeuvres by today's standards, but very dashing less than a decade after man's first powered flight. Pégoud was a natural display pilot, an extrovert who would publicly consume a whole roast chicken and a bottle of champagne before a flight. When he visited England he was *fêted* at a dinner given to celebrate his prowess at inverted flight; the tables were upturned and the courses served in reverse order, coffee and liqueurs first and finishing with the soup.

Every American promoter was soon trying to book a 'looper', though there were only three barnstormers in the entire United States who had demonstrated this new phenomenon – DeLloyd Thompson, Charles F. Niles and Lincoln Beachey, who came out of his self-imposed retire-

ment and built his 'Little Looper', an 80 hp Gnome rotary-engined pusher biplane designed expressly for inverted flight, in which he could perform successive loops and actually gain height, when all his competitors were forever struggling to regain sufficient altitude for their next world-turning manoeuvre.

Beachey soon became the top box-office attraction, earning, at the peak of his career, $4,000 a week for stunts which included picking up handkerchiefs with a wingtip, flying under Niagara Falls Bridge, and disguising himself as The Mystery Woman Aviatrix for an aerial drag act. In March 1915 he went to San Francisco to fly at the Pan-Pacific Exposition, lured by the promise of an astonishing $1,500 per flight. He never lived to see the

money. His new Beachey Monoplane shed its wings while pulling out from an 'S' dive, and Beachey fell into San Francisco Bay in front of 50,000 horrified spectators. Next day they were back, horror overcome, to watch Art Smith, billed as 'The Boy Looper from Fort Wayne', take over Beachey's act, and elaborate on it with a literally dazzling display of night aerobatics with illumination provided by fireworks and smokeflares attached to his aeroplane.

The coming of war with Germany brought an end to exhibition flying and at the same time heralded the birth of barnstorming's golden era, for when peace came again in 1918 thousands of demobilised British, Canadian and American airmen found themselves with no jobs to go to and no trades to their names save flying. Many did drift into other careers, but some, either through economic necessity or optimism for the then-black future of commercial aviation, bought up war-surplus aeroplanes which were being disposed of at a fraction of their cost and set forth to bring flying to the masses.

Joyriding operations

The most popular aeroplanes among the British barnstormers were variants of the Avro 504K trainer powered by Le Rhône, Monosoupape, Bentley or Clerget rotary engines. Avros could be obtained quite cheaply from the Disposal Board, at least one example being sold for just £20, and a complete strip-down inspection and re-assembly, usually with the rear cockpit converted to carry two passengers, did not involve much additional expenditure. Thus equipped, the barnstormers set off to offer air-hungry citizens an aerial baptism at a guinea a time, two guineas for those brave souls who wanted to stunt. In 1919 one optimistic aviation writer predicted that the potential demand for this 'joy-riding' might exceed five million people. In truth it never grew quite that big,

but those fliers who managed to corner the lucrative seaside market found themselves with no shortage of customers. One such was Alan (later Sir Alan) Cobham, who teamed up with Oscar P. Jones, the 'grand old man' of airline flying, who retired from BOAC in 1955 having flown 21,600 hours and carried 139,000 passengers, mostly during years when airliners seldom carried more than three dozen travellers.

One of the largest and most successful joyriding operations was run by Major Gordon McMinnies at Blackpool. In June and July of 1919 his Avros carried 10,000 people, each of his four pilots flying 42 trips a day, and still they failed to clear the queues of eager passengers.

While their British counterparts were busy storming

holiday beaches, American barnstormers were spreading across the nation like a swarm (some said a plague) of locusts. They flew de Havilland DH-4s, Thomas-Morse Scouts, Standards and especially Curtiss JN-4D Jennies, the American equivalent of the Avro 504. After the war, the US Army Air Service sold off Jennies for as little as $300, brand-new, still in their packing cases, and often with a spare engine thrown in. The spare engine was a good thing to have around with a Jenny, for it was powered by another Glenn Curtiss product, the OX5 engine, a melancholy device which would produce, if one was very lucky, all of 90 horsepower for its massive 434lb weight. OX-5s were so prone to breakdown for an endless variety of reasons that they were nicknamed 'failures looking for somewhere to happen'. Even the crates came in useful as shanty homes for impecunious fliers when times were hard, as often they were. 'The greatest danger in this business,' wrote one barnstormer, 'is that of starving to death.'

Aerial gypsies
Nonetheless, thousands of ex-military pilots started out to live the life of an aerial gypsy, setting their aeroplanes down in pastures where they would enlist the help of the farmer and his family in return for free rides. Everyone else paid a dollar a minute, and loved it. Most of

Above: a present-day wing-walker is harnessed to the upper centre-section of a Tiger Moth. Opposite top: a Druine Turbulent formates with a Tiger Moth with wing-walker atop. Opposite bottom: one of todays display teams is aptly named 'Barnstormers'

the barnstormers were in the business simply to make money the only way they knew how. A few were charlatans, passenger flying and thought this was the way to convince the public that aeroplanes were safe.

Among such men were Clyde Pangborn, Eddie Stinson, Frank Hawks, Roscoe Turner, Eddie Rickenbacker, Wiley Post, Jimmy Doolittle, and, best known of all, Charles Lindbergh. They were all gypsy pilots in the early days, sleeping out under the wings of their aeroplanes, patching them with a piece of some admiring young lady's petticoat, replacing snapped rigging with a length of baling wire, trying to save a dollar or two for the day when they'd get started in the airline business, as many of them eventually did. 'Slim' Lindbergh barnstormed a Jenny for two years, billing himself as 'Daredevil Lindbergh', though the newspapers preferred 'The Flying Fool'. In March 1924 he decided he'd had enough, and flew to Brooks Field, Texas, to enlist in the Army Air Service. When the commanding officer saw his battered Jenny, one tyre gone, the fabric shredded and a cracked wingspar held together with rope, he ordered Lindbergh to get it off his flying field, '*now*'!

Wing walking

To attract the paying customers to their improvised airfields, the barnstormers organised elaborate stunt routines over nearby towns—parachuting, low-level aerobatics and, most picturesque of all, wing-walking. Perhaps the greatest wing-walker was Ormer Locklear, a former World War I flight instructor. Legend has it that Locklear was flying in a Jenny over Texas one day when the radiator cap blew off. Casually, he clambered on top of the wing and stuck a rag in the hole to keep the scalding water from being blown into the cockpits, and proceeded on his way.

Once honourably discharged from the Army, Locklear worked up a series of wing-walking stunts in which he would prance about among the cats-cradle rigging of a Jenny—it was said that if a bird could escape from the rigging there was a slack wire somewhere—sit on the under-carriage spreader-bar, hang by his hands, feet and teeth from a rope, and climb down a rope-ladder on to another aeroplane flying in formation. Locklear drew crowds. He also achieved a notable first—the first known warrant for 'reckless aerial driving' was issued against him by a Los Angeles court. He died on the night of 2 August 1920, having quit barnstorming to join the madcap motion-picture pilots and stuntmen in Hollywood. He was performing a night tailspin with phosphorous flares for 'The Skywayman' when he crashed—blinded, some say, by a battery of arc lights—into the sludge pool of an oil well.

Another great innovator was Earl Daugherty, from Long Beach, California. Like Locklear, he looked for wild new stunts to draw the crowds who were already becoming bored with routine wing-walking. With the help of an agile wing-walker, Wesley May, Daugherty performed the first aerial refuelling. His partner Frank Hawks took off with May crouching on top of his Standard biplane, a five-gallon can of petrol strapped to his back, whilst Daugherty followed in a Jenny, closing in until its lower wing was overlapping the upper wing of the Standard. May grabbed the Jenny's wingtip skid, hauled himself aboard, strode

down the wing and calmly poured the fuel into the fuselage tank, to the accompaniment of mad cheering from the wildly excited spectators.

Daugherty, too, went to Hollywood, and, again like Locklear, died in an accident. Barnstorming took many lives. In 1923 gypsy fliers were responsible for 85 deaths and 162 injuries in 179 serious accidents. Parachuting was the primary cause, with low-level aerobatics and structural failure close behind. By 1927, when the American Government introduced the first federal air regulations, the barnstormers had all but faded from the scene. Their aeroplanes, often poorly maintained, became more dangerous as they aged, and the public were becoming alarmed at the accident rate. The glorious years of barnstorming had gone, but to those fliers is owed a great debt, for it was they who first brought flying within reach of ordinary people.

A living tradition

Barnstorming lives on, even now. Throughout the 1930s Alan Cobham retained his interest in entertaining the public, and from 1932–36 his flying circus put on 12,000 displays and carried a million passengers. His

Right: a Pitts Special of the Rothmans Aerobatic Team during a display. Below: one of the Tiger Club's display specialities is wing-walking, for which the Club's Tiger Moths are well-suited

legacy was inherited in the late 1950s by Norman Jones, chairman of the Tiger Club, who put together a touring airshow with all the old favourite acts: aerobatics, balloon bursting, wing-walking, even the ever-popular crazy-flying spot, in which a not-too-well disguised pilot, posing as a farmer, maiden aunt or even the local vicar, 'accidentally' starts up a parked aeroplane and goes careering across the field in a series of heart-stopping swoops and dives. It never fails to raise a laugh, though it is doubtful if anyone is fooled.

The Tiger Club's pilots, many of whom spend their working days on the flight-decks of airliners and hardly fit the oil-stained image of the barnstormers, together with professional display teams such as the Rothmans Aerobatic Team, The Barnstormers, and the Red Arrows, keep alive the traditions of the early exhibition fliers. And even though supersonic flight is now available for the price of an airline ticket, they still pull the crowds. Curtiss, Locklear, Beachey and all the others who showed the way would be proud of them.

Smith-Barry
The man who devised the first proper system of flying instruction

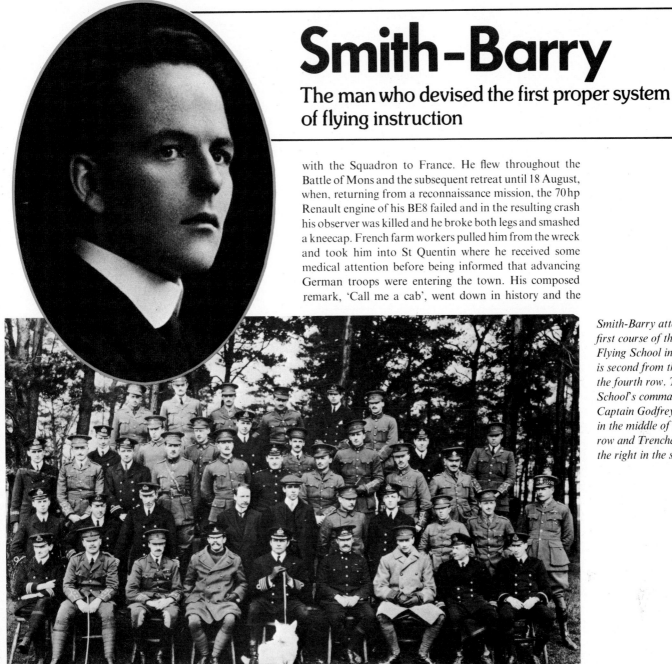

with the Squadron to France. He flew throughout the Battle of Mons and the subsequent retreat until 18 August, when, returning from a reconnaissance mission, the 70 hp Renault engine of his BE8 failed and in the resulting crash his observer was killed and he broke both legs and smashed a kneecap. French farm workers pulled him from the wreck and took him into St Quentin where he received some medical attention before being informed that advancing German troops were entering the town. His composed remark, 'Call me a cab', went down in history and the

Smith-Barry attended the first course of the Central Flying School in 1912. He is second from the left in the fourth row. The School's commandant, Captain Godfrey Paine, is in the middle of the front row and Trenchard is on the right in the second row

Robert Smith-Barry was born in 1886 and was educated at Eton and Cambridge University. He had distinguished parents, for his father was a descendant from the Irish Earls of Barrymore, County Cork, while his mother was the daughter of the Earl of Enniskillen.

In 1909 he entered the Consular Service, serving at one period in Constantinople. Two years later he returned to England where he decided to take up flying; he was taught at the Bristol School at Larkhill on Salisbury Plain, gaining his Royal Aero Club Certificate in November 1911. In 1912 he received a commission in the Royal Flying Corps and joined the very first course at the Central Flying School in May of that year. Major John Salmond who became a Marshal of the Royal Air Force, was one of the instructors on this course, while one of Smith-Barry's fellow pupils was Major Hugh Trenchard who later became justifiably known as the Father of the Royal Air Force.

When war came in 1914, Smith-Barry was with No. 5 Squadron at Fort Grange, Gosport, from where he went

summoned cab carried him from St Quentin to a train which took him nearer the safety of England.

His injuries did not in any way deter him from continuing his flying career and, although he was left with a permanent limp and had on occasion to use a walking stick, he was back in the air by March 1915 and in 1916 was flying on anti-Zeppelin patrols. He was then made a Captain and Flight Commander at the Gosport Training School. This school had several flights and the scout flight under Smith-Barry's command became, in April 1916, the nucleus of No. 60 Squadron, commanded by Major F. F. 'Ferdy' Waldron, Smith-Barry becoming the new squadron's C Flight Commander.

Return to France
No. 60 Squadron went to France in May equipped with the usual variety of aeroplane types and when Major Waldron was killed in action on 3 July Smith-Barry was put in command. He led 60 Squadron until Christmas Eve 1916 and among the famous fighting pilots he had under

his command were Albert Ball, Stanley Vincent, who was to destroy German aircraft in both World Wars, 'Duke' Meintjes, Euan Gilchrist, D. V. Armstrong, Alan Bell-Irving and Eustace Foot.

At the end of 1916, Smith-Barry returned to England and had many ideas for pilot training, having been appalled at the low standard of training of the pilots when they arrived at his and other front line squadrons. He had discovered that most of the pilots had little real idea as to exactly what the controls of their aeroplanes did, nor how they could use these controls to improve the performance of their aeroplanes and their own standard as pilots.

By this time Trenchard was in command of the RFC and Smith-Barry managed to convince him that his ideas, if put into practice, would greatly improve pilot training. General Salmond was now in charge of training units and had himself been trying to improve training techniques. With Trenchard's agreement, Smith-Barry took command of No. 1 Reserve Squadron at Gosport. Early in January 1917 he began to group around him a number of experienced pilots, most of whom had been under his command in 60 Squadron. All were in sympathy with his general ideas and also admired the man sufficiently to jump at the chance of being a part of his new team.

Carefully setting out a rigid set of flying rules and regulations, he built his unit into a most efficient training squadron. He went to great lengths to ensure that each pupil knew exactly what his aeroplane would do in certain circumstances and how it would react if handled incorrectly. For example some pilots going to France did not even know that aircraft stalled when flying speed was lost, especially in a slow climb if engine revolutions were not increased. By understanding these things and with a dedicated body of instructors who were equally capable of imparting Smith-Barry's dictates, a great many pilots left Gosport far better equipped to face air combat over the Western Front. Emphasis was also placed on training flying instructors to a far better standard, so that they could impart their newly acquired knowledge at training schools throughout the country.

School of Special Flying

In May 1917, Smith-Barry issued his own 'Notes on Teaching Flying' for instructors' courses which he then introduced. These notes, or at least their basic ideas, were to remain in force for nearly 30 years. Also developed at Gosport at that time was the famous 'Gosport tube', an ingenious but simple invention which made it possible for instructor and pupil to talk to each other in the air. This was soon fitted to all dual-control aircraft.

Smith-Barry was promoted to Lieutenant Colonel in August and appointed Commandant of the School. The school was so successful that No. 1, together with Nos. 27 and 55 Training Squadrons were amalgamated to form The School of Special Flying, Gosport. General Salmond was more than pleased at the success of Smith-Barry's school and had his training notes printed in pamphlet form and distributed to all Royal Flying Corps flying training establishments.

The SSF was now totally equipped with the Avro 504J for basic dual instruction, generally referred to as 'Mono-Avros', SSF being known as plain 'Gosport' which summed up totally the mystique of Smith-Barry's school.

By mid 1918 Smith-Barry's training system had become well established and its success was such that similar schools were opened elsewhere. Although SSF Gosport was renamed the South Western Area Flying Instructor's School, it was always 'Gosport' to the flyers of World War

I. Later in 1918 Smith-Barry was promoted to Brigadier General and put in command of a Training Group near York. He was not happy at this administrative post and was reported to have thrown all the unit's files out of a window. Quickly disciplined he was reduced to Colonel and sent back to a flying unit as a 'punishment'.

Smith-Barry sent the following telegrams to his superior the same day. 'Am returning to Gosport in Avro. R. Smith-Barry. Brig Gen' and, following his journey sent 'Have arrived at Gosport. R. Smith-Barry. Lt Col'.

With the war over, the School of Special Flying was disbanded in February 1919, having trained some 1,200 pupils and instructors.

Smith-Barry retired from the RAF at the war's end as a Wing Commander with the Air Force Cross and the Chevalier de l'Ordre de Leopold. He lived in America for some time, worked on the stock market for a period and was also a private pilot.

Ferry pilot

In 1939 he rejoined the RAF and the following year joined the Air Transport Auxiliary with a rank equivalent to that of a RAF Pilot Officer. On one occasion, he delivered a Hurricane fighter to Northolt. Smith-Barry climbed down to be greeted by the Station Commander whom he saluted and called 'Sir'. The Station Commander had been, ironically, one of the young instructors under his command in 1917. Continuing his ferrying duties he crashed in a Blenheim in October 1940 which resulted in a smashed jaw.

In 1941 he was Station Commander at Gravesend,

Smith-Barry at the controls of a captured Albatros DV at Gosport, where he developed his theories on training pupils and instructors

Croydon and Stapleford Tawney. Then he was made Chief Ground Instructor at South Cerney, Gloucestershire. The following year he was on the staff of No. 151 OTU in India where he ended his RAF career when he resigned his commission in June 1943.

After World War II he retired to India, later going to South Africa, where he died on 23 May 1949 at the age of 63. His training techniques had become accepted as the basis of flying training courses in the inter-war years both by the RAF and most of the world's air forces. The advent of faster, more sophisticated aircraft necessitated certain modifications and additions to Smith-Barry's theories, but his methods of 1917–18 continued as a standard reference until the end of World War II.

Jean Batten

One of the most celebrated women record-breaking pilots of the 1930s

In the late twenties women pilots began to be taken seriously by their male contemporaries and their activities were featured extensively in the press. One girl who showed great courage and determination in achieving her place in the hall of fame of pioneer flying was a New Zealander, Jean Batten. Coming to England when she was nineteen to study music, she obtained her 'A' Licence at the London Aeroplane Club at Stag Lane.

On her return to New Zealand, she tried to persuade her parents to help her in her ambition to become the first Antipodean woman to fly in a light aircraft from England to Australia.

She returned to London in 1931 without their support for the attempt and it was with some difficulty that she managed to save enough money to take her 'B' Licence. The licence required one hundred hours flying which, at thirty shillings an hour, meant considerable expense. Now more determined than ever, she persuaded a fellow member of the London Aeroplane Club to share the cost of a second-hand DH 60M Gipsy Moth originally owned by HRH the Prince of Wales.

It was in this aircraft, registered G-AALG, that she set off on 9 April 1933 from Lympne. In eight days she had reached British India but she crashed a few miles after taking off from Karachi in what is now Pakistan. On her recovery, she had to return to England, nearly penniless, with the help of Lord Wakefield. By this time, however, her exploits had gained her more support, and at the end of April 1934 she took off on her second attempt, in a fifth-hand Gipsy Moth, registration G-AARB, which had cost £260. This time bad weather intervened and shortage of fuel forced her to land in pitch darkness and driving rain in a field outside Rome. Finding the field surrounded with high-tension cables and wireless masts, she decided to return to England with her machine before making a third attempt.

She took off once more from Lympne on 8 May and reached India without too many difficulties, but on her flight from Rangoon she ran into torrential rainstorms and landed with

Daily Express

RADIO PROGRAMMES: PAGE 23.

ONE PENNY

MONDAY, OCTOBER 25, 1937

NO. 11,681

I flew from springtime into autumn . . . Last week I was sun-bathing, and now . . . . BY

THE GIRL WHO HAS BEATEN ALL THE MEN

— JEAN —
SHE'S DONE IT

Lucky Comb Was Lucky Again!

By *Jean Batten*

(World Copyright)

PLEASE let me sit here pretty close to you so that I can hear you ask me questions. And put me on a hard chair. My ears are still singing, and if I sit in that armchair I shall just go off to sleep. You see, I've had only eighteen hours' sleep since I left Darwin.

That seems centuries ago. You know I just can't believe I'm here near the Thames, with nowhere

FACTS

ALL the men who have put up solo records for the Australia-England flight have been thoroughly beaten by twenty-seven-year-old Jean Batten, New Zealander, who landed at Lympne at 3.45 yesterday afternoon, 5 days 18 hours 15 minutes after leaving Port Darwin.

Broadbent, in May, took 6 days 8 hours 25 minutes; Brook, in 1935, 7 days 19 hours 50 minutes; Melrose, in 1934, 8 days 9 hours; Mollison, in 1931, 8 days 22 hours 25 minutes; Scott, in 1931, 10 days 23 hours.

Jean's flight, too, was faster than her own record time a year ago from Lympne to Port Darwin—5 days 21 hours 3 minutes. She left Naples yesterday at 5.35 a.m. and made only one stop, at Marseilles.

Jim Broadbent, attacking Jean's England-Australia record as she flew the opposite way, will probably abandon his flight. At 3 a.m. yesterday he was forced down in the desert and had to ride on a borrowed donkey four miles for petrol to get to Bagdad.

STOP PRESS
Telephone: Central 8000

The Percival Gull Six in which Jean Batten made her historic crossing of the South Atlantic and established solo records between England and Australia. The aircraft has been preserved by the Shuttleworth Trust

some difficulty at Victoria Point in Burma on a flooded aerodrome. The adverse weather conditions continued and the Moth became bogged down at Alor Star. She took off from Batavia in a dense morning fog after an assurance from the agent of a Dutch fuel firm that she would find clear weather and sunshine above the storm clouds: this, fortunately, turned out to be correct. Jean Batten eventually reached Darwin on the 23 May, having taken 14 days 22 hours and 30 minutes and beating Amy Mollison's time by over four days.

Nearly a year later Jean Batten left Darwin to return to England, once more in her faithful Gipsy Moth. On taking off from Darwin she had to gain height to avoid a dust storm. This was to prove her salvation, for when she was about 250 miles out to sea and flying at 6,000 ft her engine cut out. As she was gliding down towards the water and having passed through cloud, the blockage suddenly cleared a few hundred feet above the surface and she was able to climb and regain altitude. She reached Marseilles without further trouble but here she was held up by tyre and engine trouble. Eventually she reached England in 17 days 15 hours 15 minutes, becoming the first woman pilot to make the arduous flight from Australia to England.

Her fame now assured, Jean Batten purchased a much more advanced machine, a 200 hp Gipsy Six engined Percival Gull Six, planning to fly from West Africa to Brazil. Leaving Lympne on 11 November 1935, she landed at Casablanca ten hours later and flew on as planned to Thies aerodrome 45 miles from Dakar, only to find that

Jean Batten poses on the wing of her record-breaking Gull. Her amazing navigational skill, together with the Gull's ever-reliable 200 hp Gipsy Six engine, brought her world records, public acclaim and, in 1936, the award of the CBE

her fuel supplies had been sent to the latter place by mistake. She managed, however, to persuade the local French Commandant to have the petrol sent by road. Jettisoning every unnecessary article, including the revolver, ammunition and other precautionary equipment French regulations had made her carry, she took off in the glare of the headlights of assembled cars and lorries. She soon found herself over the ocean, where she was forced to fly through an imposing array of storm clouds and rain on her route to Natal, Brazil. In the clouds her compass started to swing wildly but eventually it settled down and she continued on her way. After twelve hours flying she had still not reached the coast and had to switch over to her last tank which contained petrol for a further hour. Suddenly she glimpsed a lighthouse which she identified as Cape Roque. She had made landfall with an error of only half a mile after a flight of nearly 2,000 miles; a remarkable piece of navigation. When she landed at Natal shortly afterwards she became the first woman to have crossed the South Atlantic by air. South America gave her a great welcome and she was *fêted* in Rio de Janeiro, Montevideo and Buenos Aires. Shortly after her return to England she was awarded the CBE in King Edward VIII's only birthday honours list.

In October 1936 she again left Lympne in an attempt to finally achieve her ambition to fly to New Zealand. The more advanced aircraft made a vast difference and it was not until she was once more off the coast of Burma that she ran into trouble, once again encountering torrential rain. With the Gull's longer range she was able to fly round the weather to a certain extent but when she landed at Penang she found the aircraft's leading edges had been worn down to the bare wood. Her arrival in Darwin after 5 days 21 hours made her the holder of the solo record from England to Australia. Soon she was on her way to Sydney where efforts were made to dissuade her from flying on to New Zealand. She was determined to fly on however and after a stormy crossing made another of her remarkably accurate landfalls at New Plymouth, landing shortly afterwards at Auckland in the North Island to an enthusiastic reception.

Jean Batten was to make one more long distance flight when she took off from Darwin in October 1937 and reached Lympne in 5 days 18 hours and 15 minutes to become the first person to hold the England-Australia solo record in both directions. Following a tremendous reception at Croydon Airport she was awarded the gold medal of the Royal Aero Club. The threatening clouds of war and the advent of more sophisticated aircraft brought an end to this record-breaking era, but the flights made by this young New Zealand girl will always remain part of aviation history.

British Lightplane Revival

The ill-starred attempt to revive the British light
aircraft industry in the 1960s

Before World War II Britain was a major producer of light aircraft and these, especially the de Havilland series of Moths, were sold in quantity in many parts of the world. In the 1930s the new breed of Miles monoplanes rapidly established themselves and for many years Miles aeroplanes were to take the leading places in numerous air races. Then in 1938 Taylorcraft Aeroplanes (England) was founded to build the two-seat Taylorcraft monoplanes of United States design. Developed versions of the Taylorcraft saw wartime service as Austers and in 1946 the company name was changed to Auster Aircraft.

Auster was the biggest postwar producer of British light aircraft, with a range of high-wing monoplanes which had welded metal tube fuselages and clearly showed their ancestry. Miles, too, continued to achieve postwar success with its single-engined Messenger and twin-engined Gemini and the Aerovan light transport, but Miles Aircraft suffered financial problems and the aircraft assets were taken over by Handley Page. However, F. G. Miles Ltd was founded and produced new designs for light sporting aircraft.

In the winter of 1960–61 a new concern, British Executive and General Aviation, acquired Auster and F. G.

Miles Ltd and formed Beagle-Auster Aircraft and Beagle-Miles Aircraft. A further development was the founding of Beagle Aircraft Ltd as a subsidiary of British Executive and General Aviation and the new company absorbed Beagle-Auster and Beagle-Miles. This was a brave attempt to revive the British light aircraft industry, but for various reasons it was to fail and, early in 1970, the organisation was wound up, although two of its aircraft types were to be taken over and produced by Scottish Aviation at Prestwick in Ayrshire.

Auster and Miles designs
Beagle had continued Auster production and developed some of the Auster types. These were all single-engined, strut-braced, high-wing monoplanes with three or four seats. They were the D.5/180 Husky with 180 hp Lycoming engine; the Mark Eleven Army Air Observation Post with 260 hp Rolls-Royce/Continental–this was developed from the Auster Mk 9; the three-seat 145 hp Gipsy Major A.61 Terrier, which was an improved AOP Mk 6; and the four-seat 180 hp Lycoming Airedale. The Airedale was unique in having a nosewheel undercarriage. About 60 Terriers were built and rather more than 40 Airedales, but they did not compare with the latest United States types with which they were in competition.

Before their takover by Beagle, F. G. Miles and George Miles had designed a number of light aircraft. They were the M.114 Mk I and Mk II, respectively two-seat and four-seat single-engined low-wing monoplanes, and the M.115 four-seat twin-engined aircraft. In October 1961 the board of Beagle decided to build a prototype of the M.115

Beagle Aircraft continued to develop the designs of the companies it absorbed. The A.61 Terrier, (right) was a derivative of the basic high-wing Auster design, widely used as a glider tug. The Beagle 206 executive twin (above and below) was a development of the Miles M.218, which first flew in August 1962

and follow it with the M.114. Under the Beagle type designation system these were known as the M.218–signifying two engines–and the M.117.

In view of the time that had elapsed since the M.115 had been designed, it was decided to improve the design, use 145 hp Rolls-Royce/Continental engines in place of the 100 hp units originally envisaged, and make the aircraft a replacement for the Gemini Mk III and Aries. A large proportion of the prototype was made of glass-fibre and, because of limited experience with this material and consequent concern for safety, the structure had considerable excess weight. The M.218 made its first flight in August 1962, but the type was not put into production. Its intended price had been £9,800.

It was decided to develop the M.218 using orthodox metal construction and, much modified and with 195 hp engines, the reconstructed aircraft became the B.242X. The first flight took place on 27 August 1964 and the aircraft appeared at that year's SBAC Farnborough display. The aircraft was modified in 1966, but production plans were cancelled in 1967. The single-engined Beagle M.117 design was never built.

Disappointing sales

The first really new design put into production was the B.206. It was bigger than all the other Beagle types, having, in production form, a span of more than 13·7 m (45 ft) and a maximum weight of 3402 kg (7,500 lb). The prototype B.206X is said to have been based on a design purchased from the Bristol Aeroplane Company and it made its first flight on 15 August 1961. It was a five-seat aircraft with 11·58 m (38 ft) span and 260 hp Continental engines and, in its original form, was far from ready for production.

The B.206X was followed in August 1962 by the seven-seat B.206Y with increased span, 310 hp engines and much redesign. Two B.206Z pre-production aircraft were built for Ministry of Aviation evaluation and were followed by the production B.206 Series 1 powered by 310 hp Rolls-Royce/Continental engines and, later, the Series 2 with 340 hp Rolls-Royce/Continentals. Cruising speed of the production versions was 337.89 km/h (210 mph) and 350 km/h (218 mph) respectively and the full-load range 1593 km (990 miles) and 1641 km (1,020 miles). A total of 85 Beagle B.206s was built, including twenty B.206R Basset CC1s for the Royal Air Force, and three ten-seat Series 3 aircraft with modified fuselages. Compared with the production runs of equivalent United States aircraft the B.206 cannot be regarded as an outstanding success.

Pups and Bulldogs

The last of the Beagle types were the Pup and Bulldog. These were the most successful of all and it is a tragedy that Beagle did not survive to enjoy their success. In designing the Pup, Beagle set out to produce an aircraft having the handling qualities of past British training aircraft while being of modern appearance and equalling the comfort of American types. The prototype Pup first flew in April 1967 and was a two-seat low-wing monoplane with 100 hp Rolls-Royce/Continental engine and a non-retractable nosewheel undercarriage. This version became the Series 1 or Pup 100 and it was followed by the four-seat Series 2 or Pup 150 with 150 hp Lycoming and Series 3 or Pup 160 with 160 hp Lycoming engine. The Pups had a span of 9·44 m (31 ft), a maximum weight of 873 kg (1,925 lb) and cruised at 210·7 km/h (131 mph) in the Series 2 version. The Pup was adopted by flying schools and flying clubs, more than 150 were built. Many were exported and at the time that Beagle ceased production nearly 400 Pups were on the order book.

The Bulldog was a military trainer version of the Pup, with 10·05 m (33 ft) span and 200 hp Lycoming engine. The prototype Bulldog flew in May 1969 and quickly attracted export orders, with the Royal Swedish Air Force ordering 58, with an option on a further 45, Zambia ordering eight and Kenya five. When Beagle ceased operation, Scottish Aviation took over Bulldog production. The Zambian order was cancelled, but Royal Air Force Training Command placed an order for more than 130 strengthened Bulldogs of the 120 Series and the Royal Malaysian Air Force also ordered Bulldogs. The latest development of the design is the Bulldog 200/Bullfinch. This is a modified Bulldog with retractable undercarriage; it first flew in August 1976, was seen in public for the first time at the 1976 SBAC displays, and is due for delivery in 1978.

In addition to the fixed-wing aircraft described, Beagle also built five of the Wallis WA.116 single-seat lightweight autogyros–the first fully developed prototype of which flew in May 1962.

The Bulldog military trainer, which was developed from the Pup, was Beagle's last design. Two Bulldog T Mk 1s of the RAF fly over Castle Howard, Yorks

Fighting Test Pilot

Roland Beamont was equally successful as a fighter leader and as a test pilot

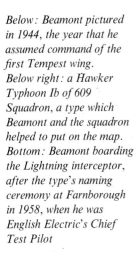

Below: Beamont pictured in 1944, the year that he assumed command of the first Tempest wing. Below right: a Hawker Typhoon Ib of 609 Squadron, a type which Beamont and the squadron helped to put on the map. Bottom: Beamont boarding the Lightning interceptor, after the type's naming ceremony at Farnborough in 1958, when he was English Electric's Chief Test Pilot

Roland Prosper ('Bea') Beamont is a man who was determined from a very early age to fly. When his father discussed his son's education at Eastbourne College, he emphasised that the aim was for his son to gain entry into the Royal Air Force College, Cranwell. In the event the aspiring pilot, who would win a double DSO and a double DFC and become one of the world's foremost test pilots, had to be content to join the RAF with a short service commission. Nevertheless, his enthusiasm and his perseverance put him into the seat of a fighter aeroplane.

Commissioned in April 1939, Beamont completed his pilot training in time to be ready for the war which began later that year. With only fifteen hours on Hawker Hurricanes, he was sent to France to join 87 Squadron which was part of the Air Component of the British Expiditionary Force during the 'phoney war'. Luckily he had time to increase his flying hours before the shooting war began on 10 May 1940.

The pilots of 87 Squadron were engaged continually from dawn on 10 May until they had, with other units, to evacuate and return to England ten days later. Beamont shot down his first German aircraft on day three of the German invasion, destroying a Dornier 17 after an exciting combat near Brussels. With empty guns he was then chased away by a second Dornier. Two days later he shot down a Messerschmitt Bf110, followed by a single-engined Bf109 the next day.

Testing the Typhoon

Back in England, the squadron reformed and were ready for action by the time the Battle of Britain began. On 27 July he shared the destruction of a Ju88 with 92 Squadron and in the air battles of August shot down three more enemy aircraft and damaged three others. Beamont also flew several night sorties, engaging a number of nocturnal raiders and damaging three.

In the spring of 1941 Bea received the DFC and was promoted to command a flight in 79 Squadron, with whom

he remained until the end of the year. He was then given the opportunity to do some test flying, under a scheme whereby pilots on rests between tours of operations could test-fly aeroplanes rather than instruct at Operational Training Units. Being a man who loved to fly, the chance was too good to turn down. He therefore went to the Hawker factory at Langley, where he tested production Hurricanes and also had the opportunity to fly the new Hawker Typhoon fighter, which was being developed to combat the new German Focke Wulf Fw190. At the end of six months Beamont was ready to resume operations, deciding he would like to fly the Typhoon which was just beginning to reach operational squadrons. He was posted to 56 Squadron, but only a few weeks later he was made a flight commander in 609 Squadron. When 609's CO was rested two months later, Beamont was promoted to lead the squadron.

Squadron Leader Beamont and 609 Squadron really put the new Typhoon on the map and, although he was unlucky enough to be on the ground or away from base when enemy 'hit-and-run' Fw190s raided the south coast of England, his pilots had many successes. Not that it was all plain sailing, for the Typhoon went through a severe trial period. However, Beamont's testing work was still fresh in his mind and he was still in close contact with Hawkers, which helped him to overcome the difficulties. The resultant improvements made the Typhoon a most successful aeroplane, which specialised in low-level attacks on ground targets, using cannon, bombs or rockets. Beamont's activities took him to Northern France, where he shot up more than 20 trains.

Tempest wing leader

In May 1943 Bea returned to Hawkers, this time to help with the development of the new Hawker Tempest fighter. By February 1944, following a period of intensive testing work, he hoped to be put in command of one of the new Tempest squadrons which were shortly to be formed. Instead he was given three squadrons and told to form the first Tempest wing (initially comprising two Tempest squadrons and one Spitfire squadron). His promotion to Wing Commander at 23 years of age, charged with bringing the new wing to operational status as quickly as possible (to be ready for the coming invasion of Europe), was a man's task, but one which he took in his stride. By April the wing was ready and in July all three squadrons, 3, 56 and 486, had their Tempests in action.

Until the Normandy invasion, Beamont led his wing against rail transport and personally destroyed a Junkers Ju188 which he found on Corneilles aerodrome. On D-Day+2, 8 June, he shot down two Messerschmitt Bf109s over Dieppe, but then his two Tempest squadrons were pulled out of the invasion force due to the opening of V1 'buzz-bomb' attacks on Britain. The Tempest was one of the few types of fighter aeroplane capable of catching these flying-bombs, which posed a very serious threat. Beamont again put all his energies into combating this new menace and his wing was most successful. Nos 3 and 486 Squadrons between them destroyed 638 flying-bombs, Beamont personally destroying 32 of them. Indeed, Beamont and seven members of 3 Squadron took eight of the top ten places in the list of V1 aces. He soon received bars to his DSO and DFC.

Released to return to the invasion front in late September, the wing flew to Belgium, being based initially at Brussels and then at Volkel. On 2 October 1944, during a low-level patrol over Nijmegen, Beamont got into action with a score of Fw190s. It was his first encounter with the aeroplane which his old 609 Squadron had overcome two years earlier and he made no mistakes—chasing one at

over 500mph he shot it down in flames near Cleve.

A few days later, near the official end of his third tour, he was invited to return to Hawkers with a view to becoming Hawker's number two experimental test pilot. Attractive as this offer was, he was reluctant to leave just as his wing were beginning active duty on the Continent. Additionally, out of 491 operational sorties he had flown 94 over enemy territory and thought it would be nice to make this up to 100. The very next day he changed his mind, but before he could do anything about it he had to fly a sortie in the Münster area. Finding an extra long, and therefore probably important, train, he attacked with members of his 3 Squadron. As Beamont flew a third run over the target to see the effects of their fire, he was hit by ground fire and had to crash land behind enemy lines. Although he initially tried to evade capture and make it back on foot, he was eventually caught. At first he went to the famous Stalag Luft III at Sagan, near Breslau, but the camp had to be evacuated in January 1945 due to the Russian advance and he was moved to Luckenwalde where he was finally released by the Russians.

Chief Test Pilot

Following his return to England, Beamont was given command of the first Tempest II wing, which was preparing for operations against Japan, but the war in the East ended before it could be sent out. He also found disappointment at Hawkers, for the choice job offered just before he was shot down had been filled when he went missing. So he went to the Air Fighting Development Squadron at the Central Flying Establishment. He left the RAF on appointment to the Gloster Aircraft Company as No. 3 Test Pilot, working on the Gloster Meteor IV which was about to attack the world speed record—Beamont testing the Meteor used for the winning attempt.

From Glosters he moved to de Havillands and then to English Electric as Chief Test Pilot, where he came into contact with Britain's first jet bomber, the Canberra. Following months of development and test flying, Beamont crossed the Atlantic in a record 4 hours, 18 minutes at the end of August 1951 and a year later he made the first two-way crossing of the Atlantic in one day.

From this jet bomber he went on to test the new single-seat English Electric P1, the famous 'Lightning', eventually taking the new fighter many times through the sound barrier. The reward for his skill and his services to test flying was the award of the OBE. Beamont also tested the BAC TSR-2, which was cancelled before the type entered service with the RAF.

Married, with two daughters, Roland Beamont's name is now assured a permanent place in the history of test flying and wartime operations and at present he is a senior executive with the British Aircraft Corporation.

An early production English Electric Canberra B Mk 2 pictured during a test flight. Beamont was responsible for testing this type, which was Britain's first jet bomber aircraft

Beechcraft

A name which has become virtually synonymous with business aviation

In the 1970s, a decade which has produced both civil and military world-shrinking aircraft such as Concorde and the USAF's Lockheed SR-71 reconnaissance plane, travelling at twice and three times the speed of sound, an aircraft manufacturing company which has become best known for its small airliners and neatly-designed executive transports is a comparative rarity. The Beech Aircraft Company was formed 45 years ago during the worst economic recession in America's history by a man with energy, imagination and more than a fair share of hope.

Walter H. Beech, who was born on 30 January 1891 in Pulaski, Tennessee, grew into a teenager with a strong feeling for flying and the adventurous exploits performed in the air by pilots and their machines. When he was only 14 he designed and built a glider using rough materials and from an early age showed the drive and tenacity which were to make his company so successful under future circumstances when other similar concerns did not survive for long.

After making his first solo flight in a Curtiss pusher biplane in July 1914, Beech served as an Army Air Corps pilot, flight instructor and engineer during World War I

and thereafter toured the United States as a barnstormer, during which period he observed new designs and innovations in aircraft construction. During the 1920s Walter Beech was well on his way to becoming expert in many different aspects of aircraft design. On joining the Swallow Airplane Company of Wichita, Kansas in 1921 and working as test and demonstration pilot and salesman, he gathered valuable knowledge and experience before leaving to form his own firm, the Travel Air Manufacturing Company, in 1924. Four years later Travel Air was reputed to be the biggest producer of both monoplane and biplane commercial aircraft and in 1929 merged with the Curtiss Wright company of which Walter Beech became president. However, after about three years in the specialised and somewhat encapsulated world of the business executive,

A French-registered Beechcraft Model A36 Bonanza, the largest single-engined aircraft of the range. A direct development of the familiar butterfly-tail Model 35, its 3·6m (12ft) long cabin seats six people in comfort

Beech opted out to devote his time to the designing and building of his own aircraft.

The Staggerwing

In April 1932 when America was in the depths of the economic depression and millions were unemployed, Walter Beech founded the Beech Aircraft Company in Wichita – he became its president while his wife Olive Ann took on duties as a director and secretary/treasurer. With a small number of colleagues, including one of America's top aeronautical engineers of the time, T. A. Wells, Mr and Mrs Beech rented derelict Wichita factory premises and began to design their first Beechcraft. Planned as a five-seat biplane with a top speed of 322 km/h (200 mph),

Below: this Long Island-based D17S is owned by a Pan-Am Boeing captain. About 100 Staggerwings remain airworthy in 1977

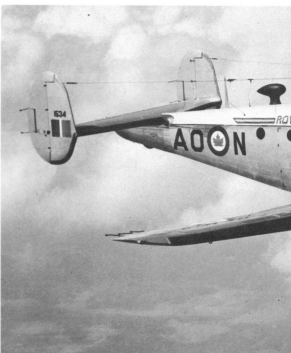

From mid-1940 all but the most pressing commercial orders were suspended in favour of building training aircraft for US military personnel and the number of Beech employees increased sharply from 235 in 1939 to over 14,000 early in 1945. Such was the contribution Beech Aircraft made to the US forces, it is stated, that more than 90 per cent of the total number of US navigators and bombardiers were trained in planes emanating from the

non-stop range of nearly 1610 km (1,000 miles) and an accent on manoeuvrability and passenger comfort, the prototype made its maiden flight on 4 November 1932, only seven months after the company's formation.

Known as the Beechcraft Model 17 or Staggerwing, the aircraft was sold to the Ethyl Corporation and in January of the next year it won the Texaco Trophy at the Miami Air Races. After another year of work to improve the basic staggerwing design of the aeroplane, fully retractable landing gear was added and by the end of 1934 the company had produced 18 aircraft.

After moving to more extensive premises at the old Travel Air Manufacturing Co site, the Beech Aircraft Company built 36 aircraft during 1935 and had four configurations in the pipeline; the 225 hp B17L, the 285 hp B17B, 420 hp B17R and 650 hp A17F. In the same year work began on one of Beech Aircraft's most enduring types, the Model 18. A twin-engined low-wing all-metal monoplane, the 18 was a 6–8 seater intended as a luxury executive transport.

Customers favoured the Model 17 in 1936 and generally business was good and getting better; Beechcrafts won a healthy clutch of air races establishing a very good reputation along the way. That same year a Beechcraft even had the unlikely honour of travelling to Germany aboard the airship *Hindenburg* prior to being used on a European flying tour.

The famous Model 18, powered by two 350 hp engines and with a cruising speed of 305 km/h (192 mph), top speed of over 322 km/h (200 mph) and a non-stop range of over 1610 km (1,000 miles) with full load was ready to fly early in 1937, but by the next year the production of purely commercial aircraft at Beech was beginning to be affected by the threat of war hanging over Europe.

Top right: the Beechcraft Model 18 in military Expeditor guise, serving with the RCAF.
Above: a Model D18 overflies the Wichita, Kansas factory which produced over 9,000 of the type from 1935 to 1969

Beech factory. Around 150 Model 18s were used as gunnery and bomber trainers (these military versions were designated AT-7 and AT-11 by the US Army and SNB by the Navy) and personnel transports (C-45 for the Army and the Navy JRB). The Model 17 also got in on the act, being used as a personnel and utility transport by both Army and Navy.

As well as supplying custom-built aircraft, Beech provided components for other companies, for example over 1,600 sets of wings were provided for the Douglas A-26 Invader which was instrumental in the eventual conquering of Japan and in the European theatre. Unfortunately, however, one of Beech's own wartime attack bombers, the XA-38 'Grizzly' did not enter production due to a lack of suitable engines. Nevertheless the war production record at Beech was one to be proud of; a total of 7,400 aircraft excluding the subcontracting and external engineering work undertaken.

Postwar production

The company found itself after the war years in good enough financial shape to tackle modifications to the Model 17s and 18s as well as the production of a new line,

BONANZA F33A

BONANZA V35B

the Beechcraft Model 35 V-tail Bonanza which was followed in 1949 by the popular Model 50 Twin-Bonanza.

Walter Beech died on 29 November 1950 just as postwar production was beginning to take off. From the early 1950s onwards, Beech increased its range of executive and private transports as well as small airliners and aircraft for industrial and agricultural use. A lease was taken out in 1951 on premises at Liberal, Kansas to accommodate the increase in production plant and in the years from 1956 various new models were added to the company's list of products. Among them were the light twin-engined Model 95 Travel Air, the single-engined Model 33 Debonair and two more twin-engined types, the Queen Air transport and Beechcraft Baron. The Beech T-34 Mentor was adopted as a standard military trainer by over 11 countries: a turbo-prop powered development, the T-34C, is still in production today.

Two highly contrasting Beechcrafts were introduced in 1961, the tiny single-engined Model 23 Musketeer and a larger corporate transport, the twin-engined Model 80 Queen Air. Beech entered the turbine-powered aviation market two years later with the pressurised 6–10 seat King Air model about which customers were certainly enthusiastic.

No fewer than 15 different models were coming off the production line in 1965, including the 8,000th Bonanza, and the 1,000th Debonair. 1966 saw the first flight of the 17-seat turbine Model 99 Commuter airliner as well as the delivery in September of that year of the 25,000th Beechcraft, a King Air A90 to the Westinghouse Corporation.

Japan placed an order for ten Super H18s in June 1968 and this contract kept the 33 year-old Model 18 production line running until 26 November 1969. It was a sad day at

Above: the distinctive shape of the Beechcraft Model 35 Bonanza, first produced nearly thirty years ago and nearing its ten thousandth unit.
Left: in contrast, the XA-38 'Grizzly' attack bomber was not produced due to engine problems

Wichita for many of those long associated with the type – 32 variations had been made from the original design specification and a grand total of more than 9,000 Model 18s had been produced for a wide variety of roles and customers, both civil and military, from aerial reconnaissance duties performed in 1938 in the markings of the Philippine Army Air Corps in the tropical jungle conditions of south east Asia to the transportation of Canadian fur traders in the frozen Arctic and the training of Chinese gunners and bombardiers in the 1940s.

The business market

With the passing of the production of the veteran Model 18, Beech expanded still further into the field of corporate piston- and turbine-powered aircraft designed to carry up

The Beechcraft Model 55 Baron was developed from the Model 95 Travel Air, no longer in production. The first Travel Air flew in August 1956, while the Baron, with a swept fin and more powerful Continental piston-engines, was introduced in 1960. Three versions of the Baron are currently available—the B55, the more powerful E55 with 285hp engines and the largest of the family, the Baron 58, which is readily identifiable by a fourth cabin window and a 4-foot wide double door for cargo.

to 17 persons and, naturally, such types soon found interested customers with varied business needs throughout the world. One particular series made in fair variety was the King Air, of which the pressurised King Air 100 powered by turbines and with a cruising speed of up to 459 km/h (285 mph) was produced in quantity. In 1969 32 commuter airlines were operating the 17-seat 402 km/h (250 mph) turbine-powered retractable-gear Beechcraft 99 airliner which was soon joined by three piston-engined Queen Air series models with seating for 7–11 passengers.

On the small aircraft front, the Beechcraft Baron light twin series was a success in both the business and private

sectors, the principal models being the Baron D55, B55 and Turbo Baron with seating capacity ranging between four and six.

Export sales have been an important and integral part of Beech Aircraft's reputation since the first sale to a foreign customer in 1934. By 1946 the export section of the company was a separate entity and during the ensuing 22 years business became good enough to guarantee a foreign sales figure for 1968 of over $29 million thereby setting a new record. In 1969 foreign countries were ordering Beechcrafts in abundance and some of the biggest foreign airlines such as Japan Airlines and Lufthansa placed orders for their training schools.

During America's involvement in the Vietnam war two important Beechcrafts saw service with the US armed forces, the turbine-powered U-21A and the U-8F, military versions of the King Air and Queen Air respectively. The US Army has also had strong affiliation with another Beechcraft, the T-42, in which over 1,000 of its pilots have received training.

Military contracts

Not only has Beech supplied the armed forces with aircraft but also with target drones. The company's first

drone, the KDB-1, was recoverable, remote-controlled and propeller-driven. Later missile production has included the Mach 4 Air Force Sandpiper with a maximum operating altitude of 27,430m (90,000ft), the rocket-powered Navy AQM-37A and the propeller-driven Army MQM-61A. Britain's Ministry of Defence ordered a modified version of the AQM-37A in 1968; named the Stiletto, it proved highly successful when test flown later the same year.

As was the case during World War II, Beech has contributed greatly in postwar years to US military strength by supplying components to various manufacturers. For example, it has produced rear fuselages for the Lockheed F-104 Starfighter, bonded panels for the C-130 Hercules transport and major assemblies for Convair's F-106 Delta Dart interceptors. Other important components have been and are manufactured by Beech for varied major aircraft, such as the Lockheed-Georgia C-141A Starlifter cargo transport, the Republic F-105

of liquid hydrogen, a cryogenic gas storage system used by National Aeronautics and Space Administration for the Apollo space programme and containers for helium.

SUPER KING AIR

DUKE B60

BARON E55

Future developments

Apart from the main factory and administration premises at Wichita, Kansas the corporation also has other manufacturing plant and test sites at Boulder, Colorado which is responsible for the main bulk of Beech's space research, Salina, Kansas where aircraft and components are built and space once occupied by the former USAF base at Liberal, Kansas where Beechcraft's single-engined range is now built.

Beech types currently in production include the single-engined Sport, Sierra and Sundowner range, the evergreen Bonanza, of which nearly 10,000 have now been built, and the Baron, Duke, Queen Air and King Air twin-engined business aircraft, not forgetting the Beech 99 airliner. Future developments in the field of defence include an

Thunderchief (one of the USAF's best-known and most effective fighter-bombers in Vietnam), the McDonnell-Douglas Phantom II supersonic fighter and Bell's UH-1D 'Huey' turbine-powered helicopter series. In addition, by the end of the 1960s more than 150,000 fuel tanks of sizes up to 1,700-gallon capacity had been delivered by Beech to the US forces and refuelling systems manufactured by Beech have been used in the conversion of Navy fighters into tanker aircraft.

Space exploration has undoubtedly been one of the most exciting technical achievements of the latter half of the twentieth century and the Beech Aircraft Corporation has been one of the aerospace manufacturers to take part in designing and building components for some of the spacecraft. Back in the 1950s Beech's technical and scientific staff were working on advanced techniques of fuel and fuels systems for spacecraft and by the late 1960s were assisting concerns such as McDonnell Aircraft Corporation with the Gemini spacecraft, the Grumman Aircraft Engineering Corporation and North American Rockwell's Space Division in the development of containerisation and transportation of high-pressure cryogenic (low temperature) fuels. Major items in this sphere included a 7,000-gallon titanium container for the storage

order from the US Navy for a specialised version of the turbine-powered Beechcraft King Air 90 to be known as the VTAM(X) multi-engine advanced trainer (designation T44A). Options include a purchase of 56 more aircraft and logistical support by Beech for a further five years. The C-12A has been supplied to the USAF and US Army, as well as to 20 foreign countries. The MQM-107A turbojet-powered target is currently on order from the US Army with expected total revenue from the Army contract expected to reach about $28 million over a three-year period. In the realm of space exploration, Beech has been contracted by NASA's Kennedy Space Centre to produce a fuel cell servicing system for the launching of the space shuttle *Orbiter 1* due to be tested in 1977.

The Beech Aircraft Corporation in its present form has come a long way from the days when Walter Beech and his wife, who is currently chairman of the board, and their small band of associates rented the Wichita factory in the midst of an economically disastrous period in their country's history. Today the square footage of floor space occupied by Beechcraft plant totals over 2·7 million and the products manufactured within the six plants are far removed from the prototype Beechcraft Model 17 introduced in November 1932.

Opposite: the KDB-1, Beechcraft's first remote-control target drone.
Above left: the dependable T-34 Mentor, re-engined as the turboprop-powered T-34C, serves with the US Navy as a pilot trainer.
Below left: inside view of the 7-11 seat Model A65 Queen Air.
Above: fastest and largest of Beechcraft's business aircraft, the Super King Air can transport up to 15 passengers at speeds of over 530 km/h (330 mph)

The Airacobra 1 flown by the Commanding Officer of 601 Squadron, the only RAF unit to operate the type. The Squadron flew only four sorties with the type in October 1941 and eventually re-equipped with Spitfires in March 1942 after two fatal crashes

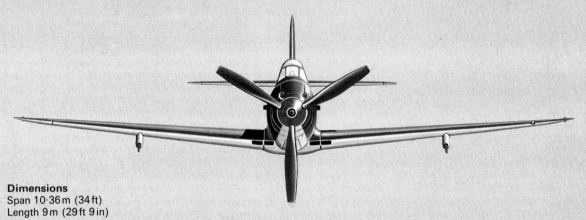

Dimensions
Span 10·36 m (34 ft)
Length 9 m (29 ft 9 in)

Engine
One 1,200 hp Allison V-1710

Performance
Maximum speed 579 km/h (360 mph) at 15,000 ft
Ceiling 9,800 m (32,100 ft)
Range 1,770 km (1,100 miles) with drop tank

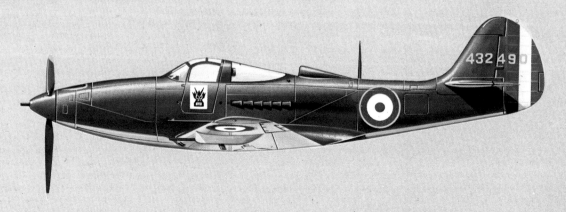

flew and he was captivated by flying machines as a boy. He learned all he could from pioneer aviators and in 1912 became a paid mechanic to pioneer pilots, including the famed Lincoln Beachey, greatest of all the old barnstorming and daredevil aviators. In 1913 Bell was appointed mechanic at the Glenn L. Martin Company, going on to become superintendent and then vice-president and general manager. In 1928 he became sales manager of Consolidated, advancing to vice-president and general manager and becoming a leading advocate of modern stressed-skin construction. In 1935 he formed Bell Aircraft Corporation when Consolidated moved to San Diego. With Consolidated's assistant general manager, R. P. Whitman, and chief engineer, Robert J. Woods, Bell hired many former Consolidated workers in Buffalo,

Since 1935, when Lawrence (Larry) Bell formed his own company, Bell has been one of the most respected names in aviation. Although the company has never produced large aircraft or famous civil or military machines, it has established a list of records few companies can match, including: the only successful fighters with its engine behind the pilot driving a tractor propeller; the first turbojet aircraft in America; the first jet fighter (defined as the first turbojet aircraft with armament); the first certificated helicopter; the first supersonic aircraft; the first variable-geometry 'swing-wing' aircraft; the first jet VTOL; the first aircraft to reach Mach 3; and a basic design of helicopter subsequently built in greater numbers than any other aircraft of any kind since 1945.

Lawrence Dale Bell was born at Mentone, Indiana, on 5 April 1894. He was nine when the Wright Brothers first

Left: an early production P-39 on a night flying sortie. The type first reached the US Army Air Corps in 1940.
Above left: later marks of the Airacobra carried two 0·5 in machine guns in underwing gondolas, in addition to the nose armament of one 37 mm cannon and two 0·5 in machine guns

Bell P-39 Airacobra

New York, and boldly ventured into the business of advanced combat aircraft.

Radical fighter designs

The first of the Bell designs established a reputation for radical design and good workmanship. The XFM-1 Airacuda, completed in July 1937, was unique among fighters. Powered by two of the new 1,000 hp Allison liquid-cooled engines, it was a long-range escort with crew of three. It bristled with unusual features. The most startling of these was that the engines were mounted above the wing in pusher nacelles, at the front of which were gunners' positions fitted with 37 mm cannon covering a large arc of fire ahead. Several 0·5 in machine guns were fixed in the fuselage. The Airacuda was costly and perhaps too unconventional, but 13 service-test models were evaluated by the US Army Air Corps. Before the last was delivered, Bell was ready with a smaller but equally unconventional fighter, the Model 400 Airacobra. The prototype was a land-based fighter with one of the radical new tricycle (nosewheel) landing gears. It was flown in August 1939 and close behind followed a tailwheel version with an arrester hook, the Airabonita XFL-1. The latter did not go ahead, but the Army Air Corps bought the land-based prototype as the XP-39 and tested it thoroughly. By 1939 standards it was impressive, though pilots were not used to such machines. The 1,090 hp Allison V-1710 was mounted near the centre of gravity, giving maximum manoeuvrability, with mount-

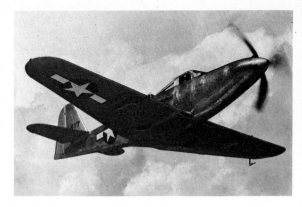

ings directly above the rather small low wing. The pilot sat ahead of the engine, with much better view than in most fighters, in a cockpit above the leading edge entered by a car-type door on either side. From the engine a shaft roughly 3 m (110 in) long passed under the pilot's seat to a reduction gearbox in the nose, driving the tractor constant-speed propeller. The nose was free for a battery of guns, such as a 37 mm cannon firing through the propeller hub and two 0·5 in Brownings above, with room for the retracted nose gear below the shaft. An incidental advantage was that the engine gave excellent protection to the cockpit from the rear.

Airacobras and Kingcobras

Clearly there were many drawbacks to the engine installation, including the weight and mechanical complexity and the possibility of the engine crushing the pilot in a

Above: the Bell P-59A Airacomet, America's first jet. 64 of these fighter trainers were produced after the successful first flight of the prototype on 1 October 1942. Right: the Bell X-2 rocket-powered aircraft pictured at Edwards Air Force Base. The X-2 featured a detachable, pressurised cockpit in which the pilot could eject in an emergency

crash. But the idea looked good, and in 1940 Bell built 13 YP-39B Airacobras for service trials, without turbo-supercharger, but with crash pylons and various other changes. Production continued in 1941 with the similar P-39C, with one 37mm, two 0·5in and two 7·62mm guns all fitted in the nose, pilot armour and self-sealing tanks. The RAF's Airacobra I was similar, but had a 20mm cannon instead of the American 37mm type and the 7·62mm nose guns were replaced by 0·303in in the wings. Originally ordered by France, these were taken over by the RAF—at first with the British name Caribou—but proved not to the liking of the pilots and ground crew of 601 Sqn. The unit had not received proper indoctrination in this class of fighter and soon gave up after a week or so on operations in October 1941. The rest of the 336 of this series were used by the US Army as the P-400. In 1941–42 the Army Air Corps also absorbed 429 P-39Ds with belly drop tank and 1,150hp V-1710-35. Production mounted, and by July 1944 a total of 9,584 Airacobras had been delivered. They were tough and hard-hitting machines, with an excellent war record. Over 4,900 were of the P-39Q sub-type, with 1,200 or 1,325hp V-1710-85 engine, armament of one 37mm cannon, two synchronised 0·5in and two 0·5in guns in underwing gondolas, and belly rack for a tank or 227kg (500lb) bomb. Airacobras saw service chiefly in the Soviet Union, where about 5,000 were delivered without charge under lend-lease agreements. About 2,000 served with the USAAF in Britain, the Mediterranean and Italian theatre and against the Japanese in the Pacific.

On 7 December 1942, a year after Pearl Harbour, Bell flew the first XP-63 Kingcobra. Derived from the P-39E, this had a low-drag 'laminar-flow' wing, redesigned tail, and improved systems and equipment. The engine was usually a 1,325hp V-1710-93, or 1,510hp V-1710-117, and armament was the same as a late P-39. None was used

as fighters by the USAAF, but 3,303 were built and gave excellent combat service in the Soviet Union and with the Free French Air Force. The RP-63A, C and G, of which a combined total of 332 were built, was used in a unique way by the USAAF: as a gunnery target. The aircraft was exceptionally well protected and was flown by pilots in mock combat with fighters or bombers firing frangible (disintegrating) plastic bullets. The RP-63 carried hit recorders and some had a bright spotlight in the centre of the propeller hub which lit when the aircraft was hit by bullets.

One of Bell's smallest aeroplanes was the beautiful little XP-77 fighter, two prototypes of which were built in 1943. In view of a possible shortage of light alloys the XP-77 was made almost entirely of wood, with spruce spars and moulded ply skins. Though it accommodated a average-size pilot in a comfortable cockpit, and carried a 20mm cannon and two 0·5in Brownings, it achieved the remarkable speed of 670km/h (416mph) on only 525hp (Ranger V-770 inverted-vee) and was one of the true pioneer light fighters of the modern era.

America's first jet

Bell's most notable fighter was one which saw little operational service—it was famous because it was America's very first jet. In May 1941 the first discussions were held between British technical staff (RAF, Power Jets, Rover and other groups) and the US Army Air Corps and General Electric's steam-turbine department at Schenectady, New York. The outcome, before America entered the war, was complete transfer of Britain's Whittle jet technology to GE, which Americanised the W2B engine and produced the I-A unit rated at 500kg (1,100lb) thrust. This was inadequate for a useful fighter, so, like Gloster with the Meteor, Bell decided to build a twin-jet aeroplane.

Bell already had a project designated P-59, with pusher piston engine, so as a cover the new machine was called P-59A and named Airacomet. It was a large machine, with the turbojets nestled under the roots of a broad laminar-flow wing. The tricycle landing gear had an extremely wide track and the pilot sat in a comfortable cockpit in line with the leading edge. Various combinations of armament could be arranged in the nose, typically one 37mm cannon and three 0·5in machine guns. The first XP-59A was flown at Lake Muroc, California, on 1 October 1942, with complete success. There followed 13 YP-59A evaluation aircraft (two for the Navy, designated XF2L-1), 20 P-59As for service and 30 P-58Bs with slightly lengthened fuselage. All these machines had the 907kg (2,000lb) thrust General Electric J31 engine, and despite their considerable size—span 13·9m (45ft 6in)—achieved speeds around 670km/h (413mph). They were officially classed as fighter trainers and were beautiful machines to fly. On 25 February 1945 Bell flew the first of an even larger and much more powerful fighter, the XP-83, but though technically successful only two were built. Its fat body contained fuel for a range of 2800km (1,740 miles), extended still further by drop tanks.

Supersonic flight

Possibly Bell's greatest single achievement, the world's first supersonic aircraft stemmed from the decision jointly by the USAAF, National Advisory Committee for Aeronautics (forerunner of NASA) and Bell in 1944 to investigate the problems of supersonic flight. The decision was taken in those wartime discussions to attempt to build a supersonic manned aircraft and this was done with no input from German wartime research. The XS-1 (experimental supersonic 1) was designed by a team led by new chief engineer, Roy J. Sandstrom, as a winged projectile with rocket propulsion. At an early stage it was decided to carry it aloft under a B-29 Superfortress and thus overcome the short endurance of the propulsion system. It had been hoped to develop a turbopump to feed rocket propellants, but failure of the pump to reach a satisfactory reliability in time forced the XS-1 to fall back on simple feeding of the liquids under nitrogen pressure. This reduced the endurance under full power from 4 minutes to a mere $2\frac{1}{2}$ minutes, making air dropping essential. Other features of the design included a straight wing of very great structural strength, with symmetric section of 10 per cent thickness, a fat body to house the liquid oxygen and alcohol propellants, narrow-track landing gears folding into the body, fully powered controls, and a pressurised cockpit in the pointed nose, with multi-paned roof giving rather poor forward view, and a door on the right side.

Initial flight testing of the yellow-painted XS-1 began at Pinecastle AFB, Florida, in early 1946, the pilots being Bell test pilot Chalmers 'Slick' Goodlin and USAAF test pilot Capt Charles 'Chuck' Yeager. After numerous tethered missions free gliding flight was explored, the wing loading gradually being stepped up to the extremely high figure of 491 km/h² (100·5 lb/sq ft) of the fully topped-up aircraft. The programme moved to Muroc (later named Edwards AFB), California, and here the first powered flight took place on 9 December 1946. Gradually the propellant load and motor burn-time were increased until, on 14 October 1947, Yeager survived extremely violent aerodynamic buffeting and almost total loss of control at around Mach 0·94 to go on to reach Mach 1·015–about 1078 km/h (670 mph)–at 12,800 m (42,000 ft). On later missions the original two aircraft, redesignated X-1, reached 1555 km/h (967 mph) or Mach 1·46. This was roughly the original target design figure of 1,000 mph. The knowledge gained was supremely valuable.

In 1949–52 Bell constructed a series of improved aircraft designated X-1A and X-1B, with greatly enlarged tankage, raised pilot canopy and many other changes including the turbopump feed to the Reaction Motors XLR-11 rocket engine. Span remained 8·53 m (28 ft 0 in), but length increased from 9·45 m to 10·8 m (35 ft 8 in) and wing loading rose by almost 50 per cent (a world record at that time). Many record-breaking flights were made by these aircraft, the highest speed being Mach 2·5 (2660 km/h, 1,650 mph) on 16 December 1953, and the maximum height 27,430 m (90,000 ft). These aircraft were followed by the completely different Bell X-2, with low-mounted swept wing, Curtiss-Wright XLR-25 'throttleable' rocket engine, mainly steel airframe and quite different design features. On 25 July 1956 an X-2 was flown by Frank Everest of the USAF to 3,057 km/h (1,900 mph), and on 27 September 1956 Milburn G. Apt of the USAF reached 3364 km/h (2,094 mph), but tragically lost his life when the same mission ended in disaster.

Work on helicopters

Larry Bell had been interested from the start in helicopters, and it was a great personal pleasure to him to fly his first experimental helicopter, the Model 30, in mid-1943, after two years of small-budget experiments. This programme got under way despite extreme pressure of work both on the propeller-driven and jet fighters, the planning for supersonic flight and the management of a vast Bell plant

at Marietta, Georgia, which built the B-29 Superfortress (this plant was deactivated after World War II, but reopened later as the Lockheed-Georgia Company). Bell's helicopter work was based on a novel and simple form of rotor stabiliser system, with a transverse beam at 90° to the blades and arranged just below the hub. This beam carried weights on its tips which tended to determine the plane of the rotor, by rocking the whole rotor about the universal joints by which it was jôined to the mast and drive shaft. After two years the system was perfected. In December 1945 Bell flew the first of an improved helicopter with this rotor, the Model 47. It was a great success and, though it had only 178 hp from a Franklin six-cylinder piston engine, it seated three people on a bench seat in a cabin like a goldfish bowl and was excellently controllable. On 8 March 1946 the Model 47 received the first CAA commercial licence ever awarded a helicopter, and on 8 May 1946 it received Approved Type Certificate No. 1, enabling Bell to build and sell the Model 47 for public use.

What followed exceeded Bell's own wildest dreams. The Bell 47 continued in production at Bell until 1962, was built under licence by Kawasaki (Japan), Agusta (Italy) and Westland (UK), and in 1977 after 31 years was still being made by Augusta. Total deliveries approach 6,000, a figure handsomely surpassed by only one other helicopter–and that another Bell product. Most Bell 47s have a steel-tube open girder tail boom, 305 hp Lycoming VO-435 engine, seats for three and cruising speed of 138 km/h (86 mph). Bell followed with the larger YH-12 for the US Air Force, and the HSL-1, a unique 2,500 hp machine with a rotor at each end of a box-like body packed with sensors and weapons. The HSL was the first helicopter designed for anti-submarine warfare, and it served from ships and shore bases of the US Navy.

VTOL and swing wings

During the 1950s Bell produced various research aircraft, split the company into aircraft (Niagara Falls/Buffalo) and helicopter (Fort Worth, Texas) divisions, and diversified into new areas. Several V/STOL (Vertical/Short Take-off and Landing) prototypes were flown, the first of which continued the company's remarkable record of 'firsts' in being the first free-flight jet-VTOL and the first aircraft with vectored jets. Quickly assembled from parts of other aircraft, the Bell VTO of 1953 had a Fairchild J44 turbojet pivoted on each side to give lift or thrust. A J69 on the fuselage provided compressed air for control jets at the wing tips and tail. An equally significant programme was the Bell X-5, the world's first swing-wing aircraft. Based on the wartime Messerschmitt P.1101, the X-5 was built to fighter standards so that the USAF could evaluate the variable-sweep concept for combat aircraft. Though the X-5 was fully successful, two aircraft accruing a wealth of test data from 20 June 1951, it was to be another ten years before the USAF decided to buy swing-wings (using almost the same geometry as Bell had chosen).

The Huey family

Bell's biggest-ever programme began in 1955 when the Bell Helicopter Company in Texas was selected to build a new utility helicopter for the US Army. Designated XH-40, it was the first American helicopter to go into production with a turbine engine–the 770 shp T53 produced by Avco Lycoming. The first XH-40 flew on 22 October 1956, and gradually developed with small changes into the HU-1, a designation which brought about the popular name 'Huey' for the most widely used helicopter

*Above: the most widely-
used helicopter in history,
the Bell UH-1 'Huey'.
Officially named the
Iroquois, over 10,000
Hueys are now in world-
wide service.
Inset left: a Bell 47G
equipped for crop-spraying
operation.
Inset below left: a
Bell 206A JetRanger. This
example was built by
Agusta in Italy under
licence.
Inset below: the military
version of the JetRanger in
service with the US armed
forces is the OH-58A
Kiowa*

in history. Bell Helicopter's own model number was 204, and the official US Army name has always been Iroquois, but to helicopter people everywhere the whole family will always be called Hueys.

Most of the early batches had 825hp T53 engines and seated eight. As the power of the T53 engine rose to 1,100hp so did the capability of the Huey grown and the mass-produced UH-1B (by this time the designation letters had been reversed) of 1961 seated ten. Countless versions followed for navies, armies and air forces, along with Model 204B civil variants. In August 1961 Bell Helicopter flew the first Model 205, with 1,400hp engine and from 12 to 15 seats. Like the 204 this was built under licence by Agusta in Italy and Fuji in Japan, as well as by Dornier in West Germany and AIDC/CAF in Taiwan. In 1969 the Model 212, usually called the Twin Two-Twelve, introduced the 1,800hp Pratt & Whitney Canada PT6T twin-coupled engine, giving engine-out safety for bad weather operation. Since 1973 a complete new family of Model 214 Hueys, powered by the 2,930hp Avco Lycoming T55 (LTC4B) engine, has extended the capability of this great family further. Whereas the original XH-40 had a total laden weight of 2630kg (5,800lb) the latest 214 weighs 7257kg (16,000lb) and can lift loads 50 per cent greater than the XH-40's laden weight. Added to this enormously greater lifting performance is higher speed, longer range and much reduced need for maintenance.

Helicopter gunships
On 7 September 1965 Bell Helicopter flew the first Model 209 Huey Cobra, used by the US Army as the AH-1 series. These are slim-bodied gunships, with a fighter-like cockpit seating a gunner in front and the pilot above and behind. Very diverse forms of armament can be carried, such as a remotely sighted 7·62mm multi-barrel Minigun turret, 20mm or 30mm cannon, six pods for rockets, eight TOW anti-tank guided missiles and a diverse array of night-vision systems and other sensing and aiming systems. The US Army needed a gunship helicopter in large numbers for the Vietnam campaign and 1,124 of the original version were delivered, followed by many more elaborately equipped and more powerful models for the Marines, Spanish Navy and–to the tune of 202 examples–Iran. Today the number of Huey versions of all kinds delivered far exceeds 10,000 and many more are on order.

Since 1960 Bell has changed greatly. After Larry Bell retired, control passed by stages to the present owners, Textron Inc. The former aircraft division at Niagara Falls/Buffalo became successively Bell Aerosystems and finally Bell Aerospace. As the leading American exponent

of air-cushion (Hovercraft) technology, it builds air-cushion vehicles for military and civil customers, as well as the ACLG (Air-Cushion Landing Gear) for aircraft. Other products include all-weather landing systems for aircraft carriers, rocket propulsion systems for spacecraft and ICBM upper stages, and such jet-lift systems as the human Jet Belt and the Lunar Landing Training Vehicle. Bell Helicopter Textron continues to be, in terms of output, the world leader in rotary-winged flight. Beside the later Huey models are produced the JetRanger series of civil and military executives and utility machines, powered by 317–420hp Allison turbines and seating from four to seven. Civil models are Type 206 while military versions include the OH-58A Kiowa, CH-136 and TH-55 Sea-Ranger. For the future executive market the sleek Model 222 flew for the first time in August 1976, powered by two of a new family of 650hp engines from Avco Lycoming and carrying up to ten people at speeds up to 290km/h (180mph). Among many other new products and projects the XV-15 must also be mentioned. A refined development of many V/STOL research aircraft of 15 years earlier (when Bell flew such machines as the tilt-jet X-14 and tilt-rotor XV-3), the XV-15 has a fixed wing carrying on its tips two Lycoming turbines driving propeller/rotors. The tip pods can swivel on the tips of the wing to give vertical lift or thrust for forward flight at speeds up to 612km/h (380mph). It may open the way to yet a further generation of Bell aircraft in the late 1980s.

Top left: a HueyCobra seen during service trials carries an Airborne Laser Locator Designator under its stub-wing.
Top right: in normal guise, the HueyCobra is the US Army's standard attack helicopter.
Above: the Bell XV-15 is the result of 15 years of V/STOL research. The Lycoming turbines, seen here in a transitional position, swivel at the end of a fixed wing to give vertical lift or forward thrust

Genius of the Airfoil

Guiseppe Bellanca was considered to be one of the best aeroplane designers of the Lindbergh era

'The genius of the airfoil' the American newspapers called him, just as they called Lindbergh 'Slim' or 'the Flying Fool.' It was the Lindbergh era that made Bellanca famous; and it was very nearly in a Bellanca aeroplane, rather than a Ryan, that Lindbergh set off from New York for Paris in 1927.

Guiseppe Mario Bellanca was born in Sicily in 1886 and he studied engineering in Italy before he and his sisters and a brother all emigrated to America in 1910. They settled in Brooklyn and it was in the basement of their family home there that Bellanca built his first aeroplane, a frail monoplane with tail surfaces sustained on delicate stick outriggers. The machine flew quite well and with it Bellanca taught himself to fly, at Mineola on Long Island. He then began hiring it out to other would-be aviators, while he developed other ideas for aircraft. One was for a trimotor and Bellanca even got an order from the British government (then at war with Germany) for it, but he couldn't raise the necessary capital.

First design

Bellanca then took a job as aeronautical engineer with a company in Maryland. With the Armistice there were no more military orders, however, and the company folded. Bellanca moved west to Omaha, Nebraska. Here he designed and built his first successful cabin monoplane, powered by an engine that he picked up in a junkyard for $35 (£7). With this CF Air Sedan he began to win a long series of speed and efficiency records—13 first places in various trials at air meetings. However new aeroplanes did not sell in America in 1923, because war surplus machines, often still packed in their manufacturer's crates, could be bought for just a few hundred dollars.

Soon Bellanca was broke again and back in New York, rebuilding wing panels for war-surplus aircraft being used by the Air Mail Service. However, he did not always stick to the original plans and started building new wings of his own design for the mailplanes.

Word of the efficiency of Bellanca's wings got about; at least it reached the Wright Aeronautical Corporation in New Jersey, who had developed under US Navy sponsorship an extraordinary new aero engine. This was the Whirlwind; its novelty was that it was an air-cooled radial in an era when the other US aero engines were all water-cooled in-line types. The Whirlwind was very powerful for its weight and reliable due to its simplicity and lack of water 'plumbing'. Wright hired Bellanca to design an aircraft of equal efficiency, to demonstrate their new engine to the commercial market. The pilot crashed

Top: this Bellanca-built Champion Citabria—the name is 'airbatic' in reverse—came first in the King's Cup air race in 1970. Above: powered by the 200hp Wright Whirlwind engine, the WB-1 had the faired 'lifting struts' which were a feature of Bellanca's early designs

this WB-1 on an early flight, but Bellanca persuaded Wright to let him build a WB-2 successor. At the 1926 air races in Philadelphia this aeroplane took every first place ribbon for speed and efficiency.

A difficult partner

In consequence the Wright Corporation was inundated with orders for their engine from the military services and decided not to promote the engine further for the civil market. They also decided that they did not want to build any more aircraft, since this would put them into competition with the other manufacturers who were their customers. This left Bellanca once more out of a job. He was soon approached with an offer of partnership by a brash newcomer to aviation named Charles Levine. Charlie Levine was 'a fellow who knew all the angles' and

---

Three of Guiseppe Bellanca's designs saw US military service in the inter-war years. The C-27 Airbus served the Army Air Corps from 1932, some of the 14 aircraft being re-engined with the 750 hp Wright Cyclone as the C-27C. Three Skyrockets were purchased by the Navy designated XRE-1 to 3, the latter being an air ambulance for the Marines, and a Senior Skyrocket was added in 1938.

---

an argumentative man, who had a reputation for thumping his opponent if the argument did not go his way. But he had a lot of money – indeed, he had become a self-made millionaire at the age of 30, dealing in scrap, war-surplus, ammunition shells. With just a few flying lessons. Levine had entered aviation head-down, like a bull going into a china shop, 'upsetting traditions and flouting codes'. He combined 'a disturbing commercial instinct' with 'a positive genius for rubbing people the wrong way'.

With Levine's cash the partners bought the neat Bellanca monoplane from the Wright Corp. Levine's idea was to bid for an air mail contract with it, but Bellanca had already had a visit from a young air mail pilot named Lindbergh, seeking to buy the plane for a transatlantic attempt. The Wright Corporation had told the unknown Lindbergh, who struck most who met him then as 'a yokel with large ideas', that the plane was not for sale. Now Bellanca shot off a cable to young Lindbergh: 'Willing to make attractive proposition on the Bellanca airplane for Paris flight.' Lindbergh soon turned up in Levine's office in New York's Woolworth Building. 'We will sell the Bellanca for $15,000 (£3,000)' said Levine. 'It's worth $25,000 (£5,000).' Slim Lindbergh didn't have that much so he took a train to St Louis, where the group of businessmen underwriting his attempt quite promptly gave him a cheque for just that amount.

Lindbergh took a train back again to New York (a long journey, and Lindbergh didn't like trains) and laid the cheque on Levine's desk. But Levine made no move to pick it up. 'We will sell our plane,' he affirmed, 'but of course we reserve the right to select the crew that flies it. You understand we cannot let just anybody pilot our airplane across the ocean.' You either sell something or you don't was perhaps the thought in Lindbergh's mind as he put the cheque back in his pocket and quietly left Levine's office. Next he set out on an even longer train journey, to see the Ryan company in San Diego and the outcome was that the aeroplane that made the first solo transatlantic crossing was a Ryan and not a Bellanca. But the Bellanca was good enough and was to prove it.

Transatlantic flight

Levine's ambitious idea was to sponsor a transatlantic flight in his Bellanca himself. He christened the plane the *Columbia* and found two experienced pilots, Bert Acosta (who had given Levine his few flying lessons) and Clarence Chamberlin, who set a world endurance record in the *Columbia* of 51 hours. There followed some amazing arguments as to who was to constitute the crew for the transatlantic attempt (this was before Lindbergh had made his flight), with Levine apparently trying to drop Chamberlin on the grounds that he was small and spindly and wouldn't look good in the movie newsreels. The truth was that he wanted to go along on the flight himself, despite his nearly total lack of flying experience.

Lindbergh landed at Le Bourget at 10.24 pm on 21 May 1927, and the world went wild. Chamberlin and Levine

Above: the basic Columbia design was marketed in many forms, including the Model E Pacemaker of 1932.
Above right: the Pratt and Whitney Wasp-powered Skyrocket of 1933. The design returned to production in Canada after World War II, when 14 were built.
Below: the Senior Skyrocket introduced refinements like flaps, electric starter and a luxury cabin interior

still set off from New York on 4 June. They planned simply to fly as far east as they could before the fuel ran out – hopefully as far as Berlin. Levine had told no-one that he intended to be aboard himself, and it was not until the plane began its take-off run and he had not stepped out of it that his wife guessed that he was going.

Despite his duffer of a navigator Chamberlin made it across to Europe. When they had used up their last drop of petrol they glided down into a field at Eisleben, 177 km (110 miles) southwest of Berlin, 44 hours after take-off. They had thus flown further – 6285 km (3,905 miles) – and ten hours longer than did Lindbergh – but they were neither the first, nor flying alone, and the fame they gained was a fraction of Lindbergh's.

Levine now wanted to make the return flight to New York – against the prevailing winds. Chamberlin was

against this idea, because he had not been able properly to plan any return flight, and he took passage on a steamship home. Levine and the *Columbia* stayed. He hired a French pilot, and soon quarrelled with him (as with almost everyone else), and the Frenchman managed to obtain a legal injunction banning Levine from setting out with any other pilot. Levine turned up at the aerodrome one morning and pushed the *Columbia* out of its hangar for an 'engine run'. After this he suddenly took off and headed for London. Levine had no map with him of any kind; and while he had received a few hours of instruction from Acosta, had never flown solo before! Almost miraculously, he managed to find London and later Croydon airport. 'The arrival and subsequent landing by Mr Levine of the Wright Bellanca monoplane on Croydon Aerodrome was the most alarming experience which has happened in

Above: Captain Carlos de Pinillos of Peru is greeted by Guiseppe Bellanca in 1928 after a 9650 km (6,000 mile) trans-Andean flight in his CH-300 Pacemaker.
Above right: 14 examples of the C-27 Airbus 12-seat transport served with the US Army Air Corps from 1932.
Right: this Model 28-92 was built for the abortive 1936 New York–Paris race and later sold in Argentina

repaired landing gear was now too weak to be airworthy. Though the *Columbia* was not the first aeroplane to fly non-stop from New York to Europe, she was certainly the first aeroplane to fly the Atlantic twice.

Into production

Guiseppe Bellanca, free of Levine, was making progress as an aeroplane builder. Despite those hard times of the Depression, he got orders. In 1928 he set up in business in Delaware with Dupont (chemicals) backing. Then the Duponts withdrew, leaving Bellanca and his brother on their own. The production version of the *Columbia* design they called the CH-200 with the 200 hp Wright J5; with the 300 hp Wright J6 it was the CH-300. One of these set an altitude record of 9282 m (30,453 ft) in 1930. The basic high-wing Bellanca airframe came in many different models and with different engines: those with Wrights were called Pacemakers, and those with Pratt and Whitney Wasp radials were called Skyrockets. (Some were powered by Packard diesels.) The 300 hp Pacemaker with the nine-cylinder Wright spanned 14 m (46½ ft), was 8·5 m (27 ft 9 in) long, carried six, cruised at 193 km/h (120 mph) and climbed at 335 m (1,100 ft) a minute. It sold for just under $15,000 (£3,000) and there was a floatplane version available for $17,400 (£3,480).

Pilots' aeroplanes

Pilots liked Bellancas because their considerable dihedral and large tail surfaces gave them excellent stability. The Bellancas were orthodox in construction, with wood spar wings and a steel tube fuselage, all fabric-covered – as were most planes in those days. Where they were unusual was in the long wings (whence stemmed much of the design's efficiency) and the square-cut tapered wing-tips. The arched cantilever landing gear was unusual; and so was Bellanca's idea of fairing in the wing lift struts so that in effect they formed auxiliary winglets, almost making the design a sesquiplane. Perhaps these faired struts did contribute extra lift at high angles of attack, but they must also have generated considerable interference drag. Another of Bellanca's proud claims was that his arched fuselage (still a feature of the one Bellanca model that is still manufactured today) also contributed lift: this is more doubtful, for if it had, it would also have generated

the memory of the civil aviation traffic officers, regular pilots, and the aerodrome staff' said *The Times* next day. After several terrifying missed approaches, Levine managed to land the plane in one piece.

For all that he had broken every flying rule in the book Levine was the toast of London. He then made plans to fly back to New York with an English pilot; while his wife returned to Long Island by sea. One hundred and twelve women wrote to Levine, however, asking if they could make the trip with him. Bad weather over the Atlantic obliged the flight to be postponed for that summer, however, so instead Levine and his English pilot set out for India. At Vienna they gave up that plan and flew to Italy to watch the Schneider Trophy races and to meet Mussolini and the Pope – it was said that the latter was the only person in Europe with whom Levine did not quarrel. The *Columbia*, however, was let down by that marvellous Wright Whirlwind, which failed on take-off one day in Italy. The aircraft, badly damaged, was shipped back to America and Levine went home too.

The Bellanca *Columbia* went on, after being rebuilt, to fly non-stop from New York to Cuba; to be wrecked by Charlie Levine again just after he had obtained a pilot's licence; and, while leased to a Canadian and an American pilot, to fly the Atlantic again in 1930. Though she had been rebuilt three times she still had the original Whirlwind engine. She was finally grounded for good by the US authorities in 1931, on the grounds that her much-

trim change characteristics, which were happily lacking. In truth the high aspect ratio of the wing, allied to an excellent airfoil, probably gave the type its undoubted aerodynamic efficiency.

The most magnificent Bellanca model was the Air Cruiser, which seated as many as 12 or 15 behind a big 575hp Wright Cyclone driving a three-blade constant-speed propeller. In this model the lift struts had grown together till they formed a W-shaped lower wing.

Bellancas continued to set records. One with a 225hp Packard Diesel and flown by Wally Lees and Fred Brossy set a world endurance record of 84 hours 30 minutes. One flew the Atlantic and then on to Istanbul, a flight of 8064km (5,011 miles). Another, flown by Clyde Pangborn and Hugh Herndon, flew around the world, making the first non-stop crossing of the Pacific, from a point 300 miles south of Tokyo to Washington State. Two wealthy New Yorkers took a Wasp-powered Skyrocket on floats on a 47000km (29,000 miles) leisurely trip via Greenland, Iceland and Scotland across Europe and Asia, without (as they proudly noted) a single forced landing–which was unusual in 1935.

In that year the models were improved with flaps, electric starters, glass windows and even upholstered arm chairs as standard equipment. These were named the Senior Pacemaker and Senior Skyrocket.

The Skyrocket even went back into production after World War II, when some were built by Northwest Industries of Edmonton, Alberta, for bush operation. The type was even seriously considered when the US Army held a liaison and utility plane competition in 1950. That contest was won by the all-metal DHC Beaver; fabric-covered aeroplanes were just too old-fashioned by then.

Bellanca model designations are, like those of most US manufacturers of the 1920s and 1930s, confusing. His first (1922) design was the Model CF. The two built as

demonstrators for the Whirlwind were the WB-1 and WB-2 (Wright Bellanca). WB-2 was the aeroplane also called *Columbia*. The basic production aeroplane was the Model CH; CH-200 with the J5 Whirlwind, CH-300 with the 300hp J-6-9, CH-400 with the 400hp Wasp. Then the CH designators were dropped in favour of letters, E, F, and J. In the mid-1930s the Pacemakers and Skyrockets began to be called Model 31–31-40, 31-42, 31-55A, depending on the powerplant. The Model 66-75 was the Aircruiser. The Model 28 was a low-wing wire-braced racing design. A Bellanca 28-70, with a 700hp Twin Wasp, was on the British register as G-AEPC in 1936–1937, being used for record attempts by Jim Mollison. A Pacemaker was also based in Britain: G-ABNW, imported here in 1932. It was seized by the Royal Navy in 1941, and seemingly did not survive the war.

The Model 14 series were the Cruisair and Cruisemaster, very efficient low-wing monoplanes with retractable gear, first introduced in 1937. They had at first triple fins; a single-finned descendant is still manufactured today as the Bellanca Super Viking by the Bellanca Aircraft Corporation of Alexandria, Minnesota–which

company also builds derivatives of the high-wing two-seat Champion designs.

Guiseppe Bellanca lost control of his company, again, in 1959 and retired to a farm in Maryland until his death in the early 1960s. Today there are *two* Bellanca companies in America; the other is Bellanca Aircraft Engineering Inc of Charleston, West Virginia (run by Guiseppe's son Auguste), which is developing the Model 19-25 Skyrocket, a fibreglass 435 hp lightplane designed to cruise at 480km/h (300mph). This is an extraordinarily high speed for a lightplane, and the design is an outstandingly efficient one. The old man's genius with an airfoil still endures.

Right: the Bellanca Super Viking, latest and most sophisticated derivative of the Model 14, is still in production.
Below: the four-seat 14-19 Cruisemaster was Guiseppe Bellanca's last post-war design.
Bottom: the Scout, like the Citabria, is a development of the high-wing, two-seat Champion design originated by Aeronca with the wartime L-3

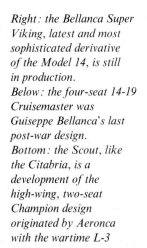

PATHFINDER LEADER

In 1942 Donald Bennett formed the Path Finder Force which he led for the remaining years of the war

The name of Don Bennett is synonymous with that of a most important part of the Royal Air Force's Bomber Command during World War II the famous Pathfinder Force. His inspired leadership of the force was due to his conviction that only by ensuring that the bomber's targets were properly and accurately marked could the full destructive might of Bomber Command's aeroplanes be used effectively.

Donald Clifford Tyndall Bennett was an Australian, the son of a cattle rancher, born at Toowoomba, Queensland, on 14 September 1910, the youngest of four sons. At an early age he decided on a flying career, influenced

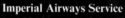

by the sights of many of the great flyers of the inter-war years such as Bert Hinkler, the Wright brothers, Amy Johnson and Charles Kingsford-Smith. He joined the Royal Australian Air Force in July 1930 and because of Australian economy measures then in force, Bennett and his fellow trainees were sent to England after completing their initial flying training.

Completing his pilot training at No. 5 Flying Training School at RAF Sealand, near Chester, he was posted to No. 29 (Fighter) Squadron at North Weald, where he flew the Armstrong Whitworth Siskin. He stayed with the squadron for a year, then applied for a flying boat course, which, when he was accepted, sent him to Calshot where he successfully converted on to the flying boats of the RAF. He then received a posting to 210 Squadron at Pembroke Dock, flying the Supermarine Southampton. His commanding officer was Squadron Leader A. T. Harris AFC, the future leader of Bomber Command. Bennett later returned to Calshot as a lecturer at the Navigation School and eventually became an instructor with the Flying Boat Training School.

Imperial Airways Service

In 1934 he entered the McRobertson-sponsored Air Race to Australia, flying as navigator in a Lockheed Vega but his pilot crashed when landing at Aleppo in Syria. Bennett injured a knee and had three vertabrae crushed. His injuries did not keep him down for long; within two weeks he was back at Calshot and flying once more. He left the

Inset left: Air Vice Marshal Donald Bennett, seen proudly wearing the eagle badge of the Pathfinder Force, in 1944. Below: by late 1943, the Force had become 8 Group and its squadrons nearly all equipped with the Lancaster heavy bomber

RAF in August 1935, shortly before his marriage. After a trip back to Australia he joined Imperial Airways, with the help of 'Bert' Harris, upon his return to England in January 1936. With Imperial Airways he flew flying boats between Alexandria and Brindisi over the Mediterranean.

Early in 1938, Bennett applied to be given command of *Mercury*, the top half of the Mayo Composite aircraft. The Short-Mayo composite was built as a means of launching a heavily loaded seaplane, the lower 'mother-plane' being a Short S21 flying boat, and the upper aeroplane an S20 seaplane. The idea was that the larger flying boat with the smaller seaplane fixed to the top of it would take off and gain both height and distance before releasing its charge, which would fly to its destination while the 'mother-ship' returned to base.

Bennett helped with its development and on 21/22 July 1938 the first commercial use of the composite was made. Bennett, piloting the S20 *Mercury* covered the 4720m (2,930 mile) trip from Ireland to Montreal in 20 hours, 20 minutes, following his separation from the S21 after take-off from Foynes. Later in the year he broke the long distance seaplane record by flying *Mercury* from Southampton to Alexander Bay, at the mouth of the Orange River, South Africa, in 42 hours 30 minutes.

When war came a year later, he was Captain of *Cabot*, a mail-carrying flying boat on the Southampton to New

York route. Two of his last civil flights involved transporting the Polish leader, General Sikorski from Bordeaux to Poole in June 1940, followed in July by the Duke of Kent's flight from England to Lisbon and back.

Theories on bombing

Bennett left Imperial Airways, or BOAC as it had become, in 1939, and was sent to America by the Ministry of Aircraft Production to ferry American aeroplanes from Canada to Britain. Eventually he became co-organiser of the Atlantic Ferry Service. In the summer of 1941 Bennett re-joined the RAF and was given command of 77 Squadron based at Leeming, equipped with Whitleys. He was

surprised at·having to fly what he personally considered an obsolete aeroplane and soon became more unhappy when he realised how little effect Bomber Command's attacks were apparently having on German targets. However, he carried out several raids with his squadron, gaining valuable knowledge and experience in the various bombing methods, and he took great pains to ensure that his crews were fully trained and able to hit the targets well. In April 1942 he took command of 10 Squadron, which flew Halifaxes and continued his crew training with them.

On the night of 28/29 April, he led a raid on the German battleship *Tirpitz* in Aasfjord, Norway. Flying into the attack, his Halifax was hit several times and his rear gunner was wounded. With his starboard wing on fire, he continued his run-in but failed to see the camouflaged warship until too late to drop his bombs. With his machine now well alight he gave the order to bale-out, holding the Halifax steady while his crew escaped. Bennett himself

Left: a Halifax II of 35 Squadron flown by Alec Cranswick, a leading Pathfinder, pilot in 1943. His family crest is seen below the cockpit.
Below: the Short-Mayo Composite comprising the lower component, similar to an Empire Class flying boat, and the upper component, Mercury. In 1938 Bennett established a long-distance seaplane record, which still stands today, in Mercury

jumped out just as the burning wing folded back. His parachute opened just before he hit the snow-covered landscape. Teaming up with his radio operator, he succeeded, with the help of some Norwegians, in evading the Germans and finally reached Sweden, from where he returned to England and his squadron, just one month after being shot down.

Shortly afterwards he was sent for by the C-in-C Bomber Command, his old CO, 'Bert' Harris. 'Bomber' Harris, together with other senior officers of Bomber Command, was aware that the only way to improve bombing accuracy was to improve navigational aids and to mark the actual aiming points in the target areas. Although Harris was in favour of each Bomber Group having its own marker squadron, the general opinion was that a special force should be created to mark all targets on each raid. Reluctantly Harris had to comply with a direct order from the Chief of Air Staff and so the Pathfinder Force was born, Harris insisting that Bennett should lead it. Harris thought a great deal of Bennett's capabilities, calling him the most efficient airman he had ever met, which was no mean praise.

Promoted to Group Captain, Bennett immediately put all his energies into building his new command, proving Harris' choice to have been a good one. He knew that the Australian's technical ability, his exceptional navigational skill and force of character would forge the new force into a useful part of the bombing offensive against Germany. Although initial results were disappointing, this did not discourage Bennett, who was determined to overcome the problems.

Aids to accuracy

Navigational aids which assisted the capabilities of the PFF included the early type of airborne radar set, named 'H2S', and the later 'Oboe', a ground-controlled system for guiding single aircraft to a given target from a distance of up to 560 m (350 miles) from the ground control installation. With experienced crews, often on their second-tour of duty, who were themselves volunteers and fully aware of the need to locate and mark targets accurately, PFF soon became of prime importance. The crews had to fly a long tour of operations, be first over the target and therefore be more vulnerable to enemy opposition than

most bomber crews. Enemy guns would naturally try to stop the target being marked, while the pathfinders' very task necessitated them being over the target area for far longer than other main force crews.

PFF began with five squadrons, 7, 35, 83, 109 and 156 flying Stirlings, Halifaxes, Lancasters and Wellingtons. By August 1942 they were ready. Following the initial set-backs and relatively high loss rates, the Force had improved by the end of the year and in the new year of 1943, PFF became a Group in its own right—No. 8 Group, Bomber Command. Bennett had been promoted to Air Commodore so as to be able to lead the new formation with the appropriate rank and when the Force became a Group, Bennett, was made an Air Vice-Marshal.

He led 8 Group for the rest of the war, continually encouraging and inspiring his men in their tasks. By now his squadrons were nearly all equipped with Lancasters, and later Mosquitoes were added to the PFF's strength. In late 1943 PFF was an integral part of nearly every night raid by main force bombers and in consequence targets were being hit far more accurately. When the war ended PFF had flown over 50,000 sorties against 3,440 targets. Bennett, who had received the DSO for his escape from Norway, received both the CB and CBE for his leadership of PFF. To quote Harris in describing Bennett: 'His courage, both moral and physical, is outstanding, and as a technician he is unrivalled . . . we were lucky to get a man of such attainments to lead and form the Pathfinders.'

Leaving the RAF shortly after the war, he was determined to strive to maintain the peace which had been won at such a high price. He became a Liberal MP for Middlesborough West and was also Chairman of the United Nations Association. Realising that, as one man, he could do little to influence world issues, he returned to flying, and was the first chief executive of British South American Airways. When he left this company he flew during the Berlin Airlift in 1948, on one occasion surviving a take-off in which his elevators jammed. Flying the aircraft, an Avro Tudor, without the use of the elevators, he brought the machine down safely with the use of throttle control and trim.

Bennett continues to be a forthright and energetic person, revered and remembered by his ex-air crews with something more than affection.

Mercury, the S20 seaplane and part of the Short-Mayo Composite, at anchor. Four Napier Rapier V engines powered it to many distant destinations in the pre-war years under the command of Donald Bennett's command

Flying Boats of the Red Navy

The Beriev design bureau has long specialised in flying boat design

Georgii Mihailovitch Beriev was born in 1906 and studied in Leningrad, where he graduated from the Polytechnic Institute in 1928 and immediately became engaged in aviation design. An experimental seaplane design bureau had just been established under the French designer P. A. Richard and after working there for a year Beriev accepted a post as head of a design team with the naval design section of the Tsentralnyi Konstruktorskoye Byuro (the TsKB or Central Design Bureau) in Moscow.

At that time the Soviet naval air elements required a new short-range reconnaissance flying boat and lack of a suitable design from veteran seaplane designer Dmitri P. Grigorovitch led to the importation of the Savoia-Marchetti SM.62bis biplane, powered by a single Isotta Fraschini Asso 750 hp engine driving a pusher propeller. The Italian type served from 1932 onwards and small numbers were later built under licence at Taganrog, and were designated MBR-4.

This presented a challenge to Beriev, who lost no time in producing a superior Russian design. Work began in 1931 and the new flying boat was tested the following year. It was designated MBR-2 (Morskoi Blizhnii Razvedchik or Short-Range Naval Reconnaissance Type 2) and the first production version had an open pilot's cockpit and open bow and midships gun positions. Power was provided by a M-17B 730 hp in-line engine mounted on struts over the cantilever shoulder wing and driving a four-bladed pusher propeller. Angular horizontal tail surfaces were mounted on N-struts halfway up the large square-cut fin and rudder. This version was built for the national airline Aeroflot as the MP-1 passenger or freight seaplane. The service aircraft achieved a top speed of 200 km/h (124 mph) and was armed with two PV-1 7·62 mm machine-guns and up to 300 kg (661 lb) of bombs.

The early MBR-2 was superseded in 1935 by a refined version with the more powerful AM-34N engine, which provided 830 hp for take-off. The original open dorsal gun position was replaced by an enclosed manually-operated gun turret set in the raised rear hull decking. An entirely redesigned fin and rudder had a sharply-tapering pointed profile. The machine-guns were now ShKAS 7·62 mm. With the various refinements, increased power and a three-blade metal propeller, top speed increased to 275 km/h (171 mph). A civil version was designated MP-1bis. It served on several Aeroflot routes, including that from Odessa to Batumi across the Black Sea. About

A briefing for the flight crew of this Beriev Be-12 Tchaika. The amphibian also carries two radar and electronics operators and is used by the Soviet Fleets for coastal patrol, submarine co-operation and anti-submarine duties

Beriev MBR-2

Dimensions
Span 19 m (62 ft 4 in)
Length 13·5 m (44 ft 3½ in)

Engine
830 hp Mikulin AM-34N

The MBR-2, which first flew in 1931, was Beriev's first design. It outlived its intended successor, the MBR-7 and proved to be Beriev's most enduring product

1,300 examples of the MBR-2 had been built when production was halted by the invading Germans in 1942. The type served the VVS-VMF (Soviet Naval Aviation) for almost 20 years and a number survived the war. During the Great Patriotic War (1941–1945) they distinguished themselves in the Northern Ocean (Arctic) and Black Sea, carrying out coastal patrol, convoy-escort and anti-submarine patrols. They could easily be converted for operation from a wheeled undercarriage or on skis. It was flying an MP-1bis that the woman pilot P. O. Osipenko broke various records for aircraft in its class during May 1937, reaching a maximum altitude of 8865 m (29,081 ft), with a 500 kg (1,102 lb) payload.

Shipborne spotters
When catapults were first fitted to battleships and cruisers of the Soviet Navy in 1930, 40 Heinkel HD-55 single-engined biplane flying boats were purchased from Germany; others, designated KR-1, were built under licence. To replace the HD-55, the Beriev KOR-1 was developed in 1935. It was delivered to vessels of the fleet from 1937 onwards. The KOR-1 was a biplane floatplane and had a large single main float and twin wingtip floats. With the M-25A 700 hp radial engine it reached 275 km/h (171 mph). KOR-1s were also used for coastal reconnaissance and during the early days of Barbarossa, the codename for the German-led attack on the Soviet Union, they were pressed into service with temporary wheel undercarriages, coming

up against Germany's Romanian allies. Defensive armament comprised two fixed forward-firing 7·62 mm ShKAS machine-guns in individual fairings set into the leading edge of the upper wing, with another on a flexible mounting in the observer's cockpit.

Development of the intended successor to the KOR-1 was begun in the mid-1930s. Designated KOR-2 and later, under the new system which incorporated the first syllable of the designer's name in the designation, Be-4 (the KOR-1 became the Be-2), the new aircraft was a small flying boat with a high parasol wing and a single 900 hp M-62 radial engine supported on a pylon above the hull, driving a 3-blade controllable-pitch tractor airscrew. The KOR-2 was easily distinguished by the very large engine nacelle set in the wing leading edge and its tall curved fin and rudder. Top speed was an impressive 362 km/h (225 mph) and armament consisted of a single machine-gun in the midships cupola with bombs or depth-charges of up to 300 kg (661 lb) weight. Despite the KOR-2's considerable success, relatively few had been completed by the time the Germans occupied their factory at Taganrog. The Be-4, as it was known by then, was put back into production at a factory in Siberia during 1942 and a few remained in service during the post-war period.

MDR-5 (Morskoi Dalnyi Razvedchik or Long-range Naval Reconnaissance Type 5) appeared in spring 1938, intended for overseas reconnaissance and patrol missions. Powered by two 950 hp M-87A radials, the new Beriev

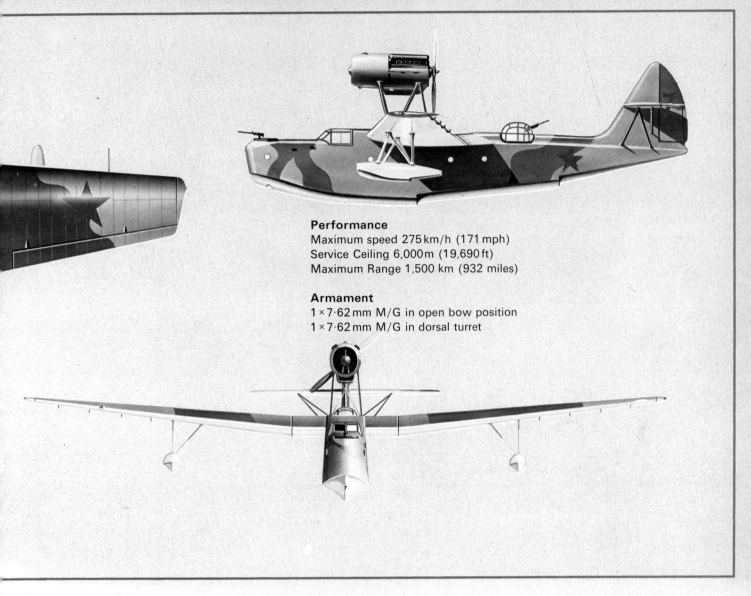

Performance
Maximum speed 275 km/h (171 mph)
Service Ceiling 6,000 m (19,690 ft)
Maximum Range 1,500 km (932 miles)

Armament
1 × 7·62 mm M/G in open bow position
1 × 7·62 mm M/G in dorsal turret

design was a shoulder-wing monoplane with a single fin and rudder. It had a range of 1750 km (1,087 miles) and reached a top speed of 344·5 km/h (214 mph). It could carry 800 kg (1,764 lb) of bombs, mines or depth charges and was protected by single machine-guns in bow and midship turrets.

The MDR-5 had the misfortune to compete with Chetverikov's outstanding MDR-6 and was rejected in favour of the latter. Beriev's own MBR-7, intended as a replacement for the ageing MBR-2 and like its predecessor of all-wood construction, was also rejected – this time in favour of the continuing production of the tried and true veteran. This decision was taken despite the obvious improvement in performance offered by the MBR-7, powered by a 950 hp M-103 engine driving a pusher propeller. Flying for the first time in 1939, it attained an outstanding top speed of 376·5 km/h (234 mph) and could carry up to 500 kg (1,105 lb) of bombs; defensive armament was two 7·62 mm guns. A considerable amount of aerodynamic and hydrodynamic refinement had been incorporated in the design.

Postwar reconstruction
The LL-143 was a large gull-wing monoplane flying-boat with twin ASh-72 radial engines and was designed with accommodation for eight crewmen and a full relief team, 16 men in all. Flying trials took place during 1947 and the much-modified Be-6 went into production at the rebuilt

Taganrog factory in 1949, the first production aircraft being flight tested by M. I. Tsepilov. The LL-143 proto-type (Letyishchaya Lodka or Flying Boat Type 143) had been armed with a single 23 mm NS-23 cannon in a nose turret and twin NS-23 installations in both the dorsal barbette and in the tail turret. In the Be-6 the nose cannon was deleted and replaced by glazing. In addition the flight deck glazing was enlarged, forming a 'balcony' with almost

About 1,300 examples of the MBR-2 were produced before German invasion forces halted production in 1942. Later models were sometimes fitted with the early version's two-bladed propeller

The first Beriev landplane design, the Be-30, seen at the Paris Salon in 1969. Designed to fulfil an Aeroflot requirement for a 15-passenger local airliner, the Be-30 first flew in March 1967, but it is reported that a spate of development problems have led to the airline cancelling its order

all-round vision, and the two ASh-72s were replaced by 2,300 shp ASh-73TK turboprops driving four-blade propellers. A retractable radome was installed aft of the hull step. Later production aircraft had the tail turret replaced by a Magnetic Anomaly Detection 'stinger'.

The Be-6 served in some numbers from 1949 onwards on medium- and short-range patrol duties with the Baltic, Northern (Arctic), Black Sea and Pacific Fleets. From the mid-1960s it was gradually withdrawn and surviving aircraft were utilised as transports, some in civil guise. The naval Be-6 had a crew of seven (plus a full relief crew) and could carry a 5950 kg (13,120 lb) offensive load. Top speed was 415 km/h (258 mph) and maximum range 4900 km (3,045 miles). It was distinguished by its high-aspect-ratio wing and another distinctive feature was its twin oval-shaped fins and rudders.

Beriev's first jet

In an attempt to meet the need for a utility amphibian, capable of a variety of tasks including air ambulance, liaison and training, Beriev produced the prototype Be-8 in 1947. Early tests showed a relatively poor performance and few were built. Powered by a single 700 hp ASh-21 radial engine, top speed of the Be-8 was 268 km/h (166 mph) and range was 1100 km (683 miles). It was a high parasol-wing monoplane with square-cut flying surfaces and a two-step hull. There was provision for a crew of two and six passengers. Displayed at the 1951 Soviet Aviation Day

celebrations, the military version was armed with a single ShKAS machine-gun.

Beriev's first jet-propelled flying boat flew in May 1952, piloted by I. M. Sukhomlin. Designated Be-R-1 it was powered by two 2740 kg (6,040 lb) thrust VK-1 turbojets. Defensive armament comprised two fixed forward-firing 23 mm cannon in the nose and twin 23 mm cannon in the remotely-controlled tail barbette. The pilot's cockpit had a bubble-type canopy offset to port, there was a large square-cut tailplane and the distinctive narrow hull was intended to reduce drag both in flight and in the water. There was provision for 1000 kg (2,205 lb) of bombs and top speed at sea level was 760 km/h (472 mph). Range was poor for a patrol flying boat being only 2000 km (1,245 miles). The R-1 was intended only as an experimental aircraft and during testing it suffered from particularly rough water take-offs and consequently no development of this type was undertaken.

Speed and altitude records

The Be-10 maritime reconnaissance and patrol flying boat was first known in the West as the M-10. This designation applied to a record-breaking version which set up a number of speed and altitude records for seaplanes in August and September 1961, attaining speeds of up to 912 km/h (566·7 mph), and setting up an altitude record of 14962 m (49,088 ft). The production version of the Be-10 had two 6500 kg (14,330 lb) thrust Lyulka AL-7RV turbo-

thimble-shaped radome in the upper part of the extensively glazed nose. The tail has a 'MAD stinger'. Twin AI-20D turboprops deliver 4000 shp each and provide the Be-12 with a maximum speed of 610 km/h (379 mph) at 3050 m (10,000 ft) and range of 4000 km (2,485 miles). The five-man crew includes two members who are responsible for radar and electronics equipment.

The Be-12 is currently serving with all the Soviet Fleets, having been seen in prototype form in 1961, while production aircraft were publicised during the Domodedovo Air Display in 1967. It has also been seen by Western observers while participating in a number of air-sea exercises. Be-12s have set up a number of FAI recognised records, including those for speed and distance for seaplanes in 1964, 1968, 1970 and 1973. A number of new records were announced in January 1974, including a speed-with-load record for amphibians of 488 km/h

jets, giving it about 900 km/h (550 mph) top speed and a range of about 3200 km (2,600 miles). Its bomb load could include torpedoes or depth-charges. The pilot's cockpit had a blister canopy and defensive armament included two fixed 23 mm nose cannon and two more in a radar-controlled tail barbette. The wings were sharply swept back and were fitted with two-part trailing-edge flaps. There was considerable anhedral outboard of the engines, which were carried in underslung nacelles. The Be-10 had a single-step hull with a spray fence either side of the bows. Four Be-10s overflew the 1961 Soviet Aviation Day Display at Tushino, near Moscow. Thereafter the type served in only limited numbers. No detailed specification has been published.

The last flying boat

The last known Beriev flying boat design is the Be-12 Tchaika (Gull) amphibian. It entered service in 1966 intended for patrol duties along the Soviet coasts and well out to sea. It also operates in the submarine co-operation and anti-submarine roles. As its name indicates, the Tchaika has a gull wing. Its hull is a conventional single-step structure and it has fixed stabilising floats. The main-wheels retract through a semi-circle to lie flush with the hull and the tailwheel retracts rearwards. There is a weapons bay in the rear hull, aft of the step, which can contain depth bombs, mines or homing torpedoes. Additionally, underwing pylons can take either torpedoes or air-sea missiles and rails are fitted for rocket-launching. There are chine boards and spray fences at the bow and a

Top: the Be-6 turboprop-powered patrol flying boat entered service in 1949. Above: welcome assistance for this powerless MBR-2. Below: the Beriev Be-10, NATO code name 'Mallow', saw only limited service

(303·2 mph) over a 2000 km (1,243 mile) closed circuit course with a 5000 kg (11,025 lb) payload.

The Beriev design bureau departed radically from previous practice – the design of military flying boats – when it decided to submit a design to an Aeroflot requirement for a light passenger or freight transport for short-range local operations from dirt or grass airfields. The first known Beriev landplane design, designated Be-30 by the Bureau, flew in March 1967, powered by two 740 hp ASh-21 radial engines. Later, French Turboméca Astazou XII turbo-props were fitted, but a series of pre-production aircraft had Soviet Glushenkov TVD-10 970 shp turboprops.

The Be-30 was intended for one-man operation, carrying 15 passengers or the equivalent weight in freight. Top speed was reported as 489 km/h (304 mph) and cruising speed as 460 km/h (286 mph). The Be-30 has not proved a success, however, having poor flying qualities and difficult development problems. As a result, it is reported that all work on the type has been discontinued and an Aeroflot production order cancelled.

It is not known whether any Soviet policy decision has been taken about future flying boat or amphibian development and it may well be that new marine aircraft designs are on the way. What is known is that Georgii M. Beriev is honoured in Soviet naval and aviation circles as one of the relatively few survivors of the post-revolutionary generation of aircraft designers who has lived on to practice his art into the 1970s.

OPERATION PLAINFARE

The air supply of blockaded Berlin in 1948 and 1949

The first time that a complete military force was kept supplied by air communications alone was in 1944 during the Burma campaign when a whole division of the 'forgotten' army in the Arakan, cut off from all surface supply routes, had to rely totally on air support to fight off powerful Japanese assaults and did so for several weeks until relieved by other forces. Four years later one of the largest-scale airborne aid operations in aviation history came into effect. The Berlin Airlift, which took place over a 17-month period from 1948, was initiated to prevent the city of Berlin from falling into Russian hands after the USSR imposed a blockade on all supplies entering the city from the West by surface transport routes.

Although a complete Soviet blockade did not begin until 24 June 1948, as early as January of that year the Russians were harassing communications and travellers between the Soviet zone of the city and the other three sectors which were controlled (as a result of the agreement

between the four powers) by the United States, Britain and France.

The situation had worsened considerably by the end of March and the United States authorities had been given an ultimatum by the USSR that they should submit all military shipments entering Berlin to Soviet investigation. The Americans refused to be browbeaten in this manner and defied the Russians for 11 days from 1 April by flying nearly 330 tons of supplies into the city. However, Soviet tactics continued to hinder the daily flow of around 12,000 tons of supplies which, under normal conditions, would have been sent into Berlin from the western zones of Germany by rail, road and waterway. By this time the British were seriously having to consider contingency plans in case the Russians introduced a complete surface

blockade. By the middle of June that fear had been almost totally confirmed as waterborne transport was almost nil, the railways had ceased to operate and road transport had thinned out to just one route which entailed the use of a hand-operated ferry across the River Elbe.

The RAF joins operations
On 19 June 1948, five days before the total Russian obstruction of ground-transported supplies came into effect, the BAFO (British Air Forces of Occupation) began to organise the first of the British code-named airlift operations. Called Operation Knicker, it began in earnest on 28 June with 13 Douglas Dakotas from RAF Transport Command delivering around 44 tons of food over a 24-hour period to the $2\frac{1}{4}$-million citizens of Berlin.

Short Sunderland flying boats operating from the River Elbe to the Havel Lake carried over 4,800 tons of freight between July and December 1948, their loads including vital supplies of salt

Right: the fleet of Douglas C-47s, operational from the beginning of the Airlift, numbered 105 by July. The aircraft was withdrawn in September in favour of the more efficient C-54 Skymaster and the Fairchild C-82 Packet.

Below right: German civilians disembarking from a Douglas Dakota. The RAF evacuated 50,000 people, most of them children, on their return flights from Berlin to western Germany

Six days previously, on 22 June, the United States Air Force (Europe) had begun to fly in supplies to US personnel in the city.

On the day following their absolute ban on communications between Berlin and the West, the Russians then declared that they would not supply any food to West Berlin and food therefore became the immediate priority for the airlift forces. The official date for the start of the Berlin Airlift was 26 June and the daily tonnage of supplies entering the city by air planned to be a minimum of 4,500. Four days later the British effort had swelled to include more aircraft and crews brought in from British stations around the world and Operation Knicker was renamed Operation Carter Paterson.

The first day of July saw 54 Dakotas from 38 and 46 Groups and 40 Avro Yorks from 47 Group arrive in Germany as well as a fair number of civil aircraft, many of which were converted bombers. Also included in the RAF operation were Sunderland flying boats acquired from Coastal Command, which flew from the River Elbe near Hamburg to the Havel Lake near the British-controlled airfield at Gatow. Meanwhile the Americans were successfully running the US Airlift Task Force and soon both the British and American operations were renamed Plainfare and Vittles respectively.

Air traffic congestion

Three air corridors, each 20 miles wide and with a ceiling of up to 3050m (10,000 feet), led from Frankfurt in the south (US zone), Hannover in central Germany and Hamburg in the north (British zone) to airfields in the British, American and French sectors of the city. Along these overcrowded corridors flew an ever-increasing number of both military and civil transport aircraft and when the airlift was in full swing there was understandably a good deal of congestion at all operational airports, with take-offs and landings at Gatow, for example, every couple of minutes. Work went on round the clock unloading supplies from fully loaded and occasionally overloaded aircraft. Emergency lighting equipment was brought into use to facilitate easier night working and runways were extended to cope with aeroplanes and tonnages of cargo for which they had not been designed.

Although the British effort was nothing short of magnificent, it was the USAF which carried the greater amount of cargo because it possessed a considerably larger fleet of transport aircraft. As against the RAF's

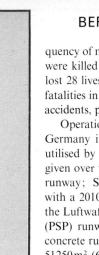

quency of movements at the airfields. Less than 70 people were killed as a direct result of the airlift; the US forces lost 28 lives in 11 fatal crashes, the British forces had 25 fatalities in five crashes, five people were killed in ground accidents, plus some German personnel fatalities.

Operational airfields in the British zone of West Germany included the following: Fassberg, which was utilised by the RAF for Plainfare in July 1948 and later given over to the USAF, had a 1830m (6,000ft) concrete runway; Schleswigland, an ex-Luftwaffe fighter base with a 2010m (6,600ft) runway; Celle, formerly used by the Luftwaffe, which started with a pierced steel planking (PSP) runway and was rebuilt with a 1650m (5,400ft) concrete runway and had the additional facility of about 51250m² (61,450sqyd) of hard-standing area; Lübeck, a former Ju-88 night fighter station with a concrete runway of 1830m (6,000ft); Wunstorf, which was used by RAF fighters until 1948, when June of that year brought the arrival of the airlift Dakotas and where there were two 1830m (6,000ft) runways; Fühlsbuttel, Hamburg's civil

Dakotas, Yorks and Sunderlands, the USAF operated Douglas Dakota C-47s and C-54s and by September 1948 the C-47s were withdrawn to give prominence to the more efficient C-54 Skymaster and some Fairchild C-82 Packets. The US Navy also contributed to the effort, and between November 1948 and July 1949 its transport squadrons VR-6 and VR-8 airlifted nearly 130,000 tons. Reinforcements for the US Navy squadrons came from the Pacific and those for the USAF Task Force from areas like Alaska, Hawaii, Guam, Japan and Panama.

British-operated aircraft were frequently responsible for carrying the more awkward cargoes which took longer to manoeuvre and it was British civil aircraft which eventually carried all the liquid fuel – the first such delivery being made by a Lancastrian of Flight Refuelling which flew into Berlin on 27 July 1948 from its base at Tarrant Rushton, in Dorset, with a load of motor transport (MT) fuel. The liquid fuel carriers included 17 Haltons, 14 Lancastrians, seven Tudors and two Liberators.

On 15 October the Air Force of Britain and the United States joined up to form the Combined Air Lift Task Force (CALTF) which had an American, Major-General Tunner, as its supreme commander and an RAF officer, Air Commodore John Merer, as deputy commander. Air Commodore Merer was also commander of the RAF's Plainfare operation which carried a variety of cargoes including coal (which accounted for the highest tonnage), generators for power-stations, newsprint, food, clothing, main and oil. In order to save time after landing at one of the busy airports, crews would often radio ahead to inform those on the ground of the exact nature of the cargo they were carrying so that facilities and specialised unloading equipment could be made ready in advance for speedy handling.

Commonwealth participation

The RAF was backed up by crews from a Royal Australian Air Force squadron, a Royal New Zealand Air Force group and a squadron from the South African Air Force. The hard-working Dakotas and Yorks carried a total of over 26,400 tons during the operation while the Sunderland flying boats were only able to operate from July until December 1948 when the weather conditions worsened and the Havel Lake iced up. The RAF also operated the Handley Page Hastings, which joined the airlift in November 1948. The accident rate connected with airlift operations was not high considering the complexity and fre-

A map showing flight paths and airfields used during the Berlin Airlift, which began on 26 June 1948 and continued for 17 months. The airlift cost a total of $224,000,000 and over two million tons were airlifted into Berlin

airport and the last airfield to be acquired for airlift use (a 1830m [6,000ft] runway was completed by December 1948); and finally Finkenwerder, the flying-boat base on the River Elbe near Hamburg, where the conditions were not good enough to permit flying outside daylight hours.

Airfield development

One of the most famous West Berlin airlift airfields was Gatow in the British sector, close to the Havel Lake, which

Above: the US Navy Air Transport Squadron VR6 at Rhein/Main flew R5D Skymasters during the Airlift and are pictured above in the crew room on the day that the blockade was lifted. Below: seven squadrons of Yorks took part in the Airlift, flying nearly 230,000 tons of supplies to the city—about half of the RAF's total contribution

had a concrete runway extended to 1830m (6,000ft) and a PSP runway extended to the same length. Eight large underground tanks were used for storing liquid fuel discharged from incoming tanker aircraft and there was an unloading apron of about 7250m (8,670sq yd). The biggest and most important airfield used during the whole airlift operation was that at Rhein/Main near Frankfurt in the American zone. A former Luftwaffe base, it was once badly damaged by allied bombs but with a runway of 1830m (6,000ft) plus a brand new one of 2130m (7,000ft), it saw many departures of USAF aircraft on the direct run north to Berlin. One of the first bases to be pressed into airlift service by the USAF was Wiesbaden, the main Luftwaffe fighter station during the war, with a 1680m (5,500ft) runway. Wiesbaden's runway was later extended to 2130m (7,000ft).

The main US airfield in West Berlin was Tempelhof, which also served as the city's main airport. It was well endowed with facilities, including two parallel runways (constructed during the airlift) of 1750m (5,750ft) and 1875m (6,150ft) plus a 1520m (5,000ft) PSP runway, and a seven-storey underground administration and operations headquarters which, during the war, had been used as both a hospital and an aircraft factory. Tempelhof, however, had a hazard as regards airlift flying and this was a difficult approach due to the presence of high buildings nearby. When the traffic through Tempelhof

increased so much that another airport became necessary, the Americans set to work and within three months had cleared away a large wooded area at Tegel in the French sector and built a completely new airfield. Intended to receive parachute-dropped supplies, the Tegel base had a 1680m (5,500ft) runway completed in August 1948 and the airfield was operational by December of that year.

Many humorous stories and anecdotes have circulated around the activities connected with the airlift and a rather well-known one which shows the camaraderie between the British and US personnel is that of the American pilot who spotted a Bristol Wayfarer in the Hamburgh air corridor and radioed Gatow to find out what the ancient-looking contraption was. Told it was a Wayfarer, he misheard and jokingly suggested that by bringing in the *Mayflower* the British were well and truly throwing everything they had into the effort!

Total deliveries by the USAF amounted to 1,783,572·7 tons flown into Berlin between June 1948 and September 1949 with more than 500,000 flying hours; the RAF delivered 394,509·0 tons and 147,727·0 tons were carried by civil aircraft. Total tonnage amounted to 2,325,808·7.

Blockade lifted

The Berlin Airlift was remarkable in many ways, not least for the tremendous resolve, determination and energy shown by the British and Americans in delivering, at the operation's height, an average of 5,000 tons daily during the gruelling winter of 1948–49 which the Russians thought had doomed the whole exercise to failure. The development of radar scanning made considerable advances during the airlift and by the time the operation came to an end in October 1949 (the Russian blockade was lifted on 12 May 1949) much more was known about the use of radar for such purposes.

However, deficiencies also came to light, one of which, on the British side, was the fact that the UK aircraft industry had concentrated heavily during the war years on the production of bomber and fighter aircraft to the exclusion of transport aeroplanes. The US aircraft companies, however, had steadily manufactured long-range transports and were able to bridge the gap successfully when the occasion demanded. The US transport fleet, as demonstrated by the C-54 Skymaster, was able to carry standardised loads more easily, thus streamlining the US side of the lift by a fair margin. It is hardly surprising, therefore, that the variety and diversity of the aircraft employed in the British effort gave rise to comments like the friendly '*Mayflower*' quip.